Kim Schaefer's
Calendar
Runners

12 Appliqué Projects
with Bonus Place Mat & Napkin Designs

C&T PUBLISHING

Text copyright © 2013 by Kim Schaefer

Photography and Artwork copyright © 2013 by C&T Publishing, Inc.

Publisher: Amy Marson

Creative Director: Gailen Runge

Art Director: Kristy Zacharias

Editor: Lynn Koolish

Technical Editors: Helen Frost and Sandy Peterson

Cover Designer: April Mostek

Pattern Pack Designer: Kerry Graham

Production Coordinator: Zinnia Heinzmann

Production Editor: Alice Mace Nakanishi

Illustrator: Wendy Mathson

Photography by Christina Carty-Francis and Diane Pedersen of C&T Publishing, Inc., unless otherwise noted

Published by C&T Publishing, Inc., P.O. Box 1456, Lafayette, CA 94549

General Instructions

Appliqué

The appliqué instructions are for fusible web with machine appliqué. If you prefer a different appliqué method, you will need to add seam allowances to the appliqué pieces.

The appliqué patterns have been drawn in reverse. A lightweight paper-backed fusible web works best for machine appliqué. Choose your favorite fusible web and follow the manufacturer's directions.

Preparing the Appliqué

1. Trace all parts of the appliqué design on the paper side of the fusible web. Trace each layer of the design separately. For example, all the petals on a flower are traced as a single piece and the center as another. Whenever 2 shapes in the design butt together, overlap them by about ⅛" to prevent any gaps between them. When tracing the shapes, extend the underlapped edge ⅛" beyond the drawn edge in the pattern. Write the pattern number on each traced shape.

2. Cut around the appliqué shapes, leaving a ¼" margin around each piece.

3. Iron each fusible web shape to the wrong side of the appropriate fabric. Cut on the drawn lines and peel the paper backing from the fusible web. A thin layer of fusible web will remain on the wrong side of the fabric. This will adhere the appliqué pieces to the backgrounds when ironed.

Fusing and Stitching the Appliqué

1. Position the appliqué pieces on the backgrounds. Press with an iron to fuse in place.

2. Machine stitch around the appliqué pieces using a zigzag, satin, or blanket stitch. Stitch additional lines as desired to add detail.

Making the Pieced Runner

1. Sew the 1½" × 10½" lattice strips between and on the ends of the 10½" × 10½" appliqué block backgrounds. Press.

2. For the side inner borders, cut 3 strips 1½" × width of fabric. Piece strips together with diagonal seams and trim to make 2 strips 56½" long.

3. Sew the 1½" × 56½" side inner borders to the runner top.

4. Arrange and sew together 2 rows of 14 squares 4½" × 4½" for each of the side borders. Press.

5. Sew the 2 side borders to the runner top. Press toward the borders.

6. Arrange and sew together 2 rows of 5 squares 4½" × 4½" for each of the end borders. Press.

7. Sew the 2 end borders to the runner top. Press toward the borders.

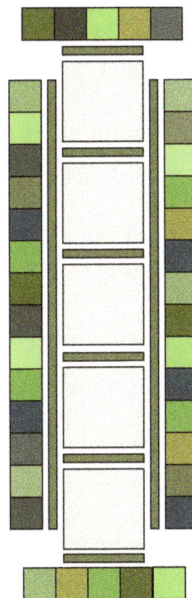

TIP For easier handling, appliqué the border motifs to the border squares before sewing them together.

Making the Place Mat

1. Sew 2 strips 1½" × 10½" to the sides of the 10½" × 10½" appliqué block background. Press.

2. Sew 2 strips 1½" × 12½" to the top and bottom of the background. Press.

3. Arrange and sew together 2 rows of 3 squares 4½" × 4½" for each of the side borders. Press.

4. Sew the 2 side borders to the place mat. Press toward the borders.

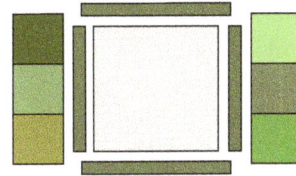

Finishing

1. Layer the runner / place mat: Cut the batting and backing pieces 2"–4" larger than the tops. Place the pressed backing down first with the right side facing down. Place the batting over the backing and the runner or place mat top on top. Make sure everything is flat and smooth and that the top is centered over the batting and backing. Baste or pin.

2. Quilt as desired.

3. Bind the runner or place mat using your preferred method.

Making the Napkins

Using scraps, fuse and stitch your selected appliqué motif to a premade napkin, or make your own napkins from fabric that matches the runner or place mats.

Snowman Runner (20½" × 64½")

Place Mat (20½" × 12½")

Made by Kim Schaefer
Quilted by Diane Minkley of Patched Works, Inc.

Snowflake Napkin

Materials and Cutting

Appliqué patterns are on pattern page P1. Refer to page 3 for preparing the appliqué.

MATERIALS	RUNNER		PLACE MAT	
Reds	⅔ yard total assorted	Cut 5 squares 10½" × 10½" for appliqué block backgrounds. Cut 7 using appliqué piece 8.	1 fat quarter	Cut 1 square 10½" × 10½" for appliqué block background.
Black-and-white print	⅓ yard	Cut 6 rectangles 1½" × 10½" for lattice pieces and 2 strips 1½" × 56½" for side inner borders.	⅛ yard	Cut 2 rectangles 1½" × 10½" for side inner borders and 2 rectangles 1½" × 12½" for top and bottom inner borders.
Blacks	1 yard total assorted	Cut 38 squares 4½" × 4½" for pieced border. Cut 5 each using appliqué pieces 2 and 5. Cut 10 using appliqué piece 6.	¼ yard total assorted	Cut 6 squares 4½" × 4½" for pieced border. Cut 1 each using appliqué pieces 2 and 5. Cut 2 using appliqué piece 6.
Lights	½ yard total assorted	Cut 5 using appliqué piece 1. Cut 11 using appliqué piece 7.	¼ yard total assorted	Cut 1 using appliqué piece 1. Cut 3 using appliqué piece 7.
Oranges, golds, purples, and blues	¼ yard total assorted	Cut 5 using appliqué piece 3 (from golds). Cut 5 using appliqué piece 4 (from oranges). Cut 20 using appliqué piece 8.	⅛ yard total assorted	Cut 1 using appliqué piece 3 (from gold). Cut 1 using appliqué piece 4 (from orange). Cut 3 using appliqué piece 8.
Backing and binding	2 yards		½ yard	
Batting	24" × 68"		16" × 24"	
Paper-backed fusible web	2½ yards		½ yard	

Make the Runner and Place Mat

Refer to page 3 for general piecing and appliqué instructions.

1. Make the pieced background.

2. Fuse and stitch the appliqué pieces to the backgrounds and border squares.

3. Make the pieced borders and sew them to the runner / place mat top.

4. Layer, quilt, and bind the runner / place mat.

February

Heart Napkin

Made by Kim Schaefer
Quilted by Diane Minkley of Patched Works, Inc.

Materials and Cutting

Appliqué patterns are on pattern page P2. Refer to page 3 for preparing the appliqué.

MATERIALS	RUNNER		PLACE MAT	
Lights	⅔ yard total assorted	Cut 5 squares 10½″ × 10½″ for appliqué block backgrounds.	1 fat quarter	Cut 1 square 10½″ × 10½″ for appliqué block background.
Pink-and-red print	⅓ yard	Cut 6 rectangles 1½″ × 10½″ for lattice pieces and 2 strips 1½″ × 56½″ for side inner borders.	⅛ yard	Cut 2 rectangles 1½″ × 10½″ for side inner borders and 2 rectangles 1½″ × 12½″ for top and bottom inner borders.
Pinks	2 yards total assorted	Cut 38 squares 4½″ × 4½″ for pieced border. Cut 5 each using appliqué pieces 1 and 2. Cut 7 each using appliqué pieces 3 and 4. Cut 24 using appliqué piece 5.	½ yard total assorted	Cut 6 squares 4½″ × 4½″ for pieced border. Cut 1 each using appliqué pieces 1 and 2. Cut 2 using appliqué piece 3. Cut 1 using appliqué piece 4. Cut 3 using appliqué piece 5.
Backing and binding	2 yards		½ yard	
Batting	24″ × 68″		16″ × 24″	
Paper-backed fusible web	2½ yards		½ yard	

Make the Runner and Place Mat

Refer to page 3 for general piecing and appliqué instructions.

1. Make the pieced background.

2. Fuse and stitch the appliqué pieces to the backgrounds and border squares.

3. Make the pieced borders and sew them to the runner / place mat top.

4. Layer, quilt, and bind the runner / place mat.

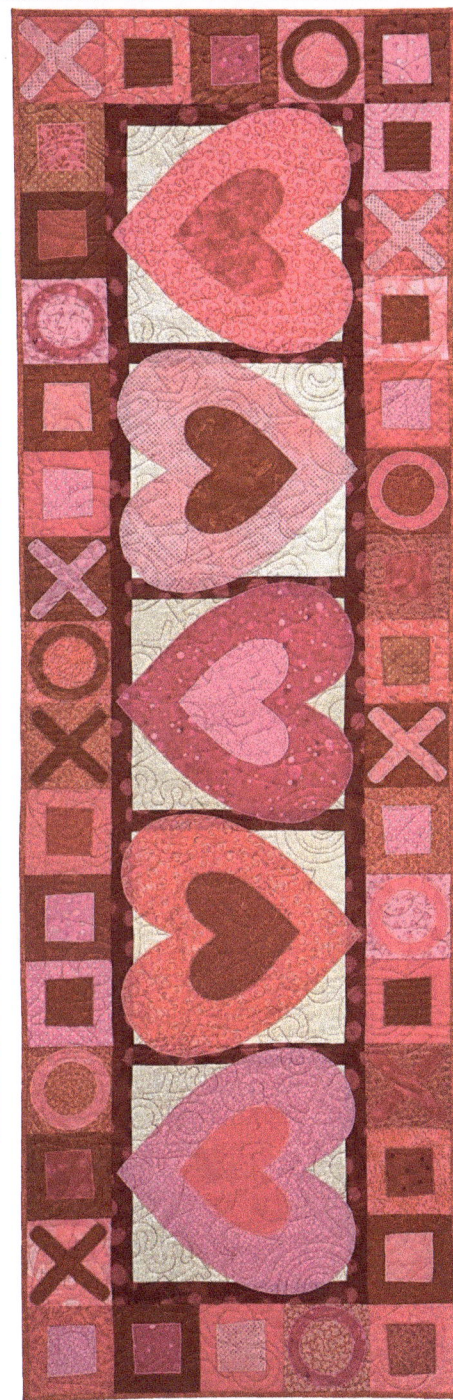

Heart Runner (20½″ × 64½″)

Place Mat (20½″ × 12½″)

March

Made by Kim Schaefer
Quilted by Diane Minkley of Patched Works, Inc.

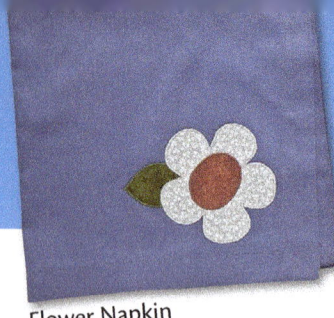

Flower Napkin

Materials and Cutting

Appliqué patterns are on pattern page P3. Refer to page 3 for preparing the appliqué.

MATERIALS	RUNNER		PLACE MAT	
Medium blue	⅔ yard	Cut 5 squares 10½″ × 10½″ for appliqué block backgrounds.	1 fat quarter	Cut 1 square 10½″ × 10½″ for appliqué block background.
Blue dot print	⅓ yard	Cut 6 rectangles 1½″ × 10½″ for lattice pieces and 2 strips 1½″ × 56½″ for side inner borders.	⅛ yard	Cut 2 rectangles 1½″ × 10½″ for side inner borders and 2 rectangles 1½″ × 12½″ for top and bottom inner borders.
Dark blues	⅔ yard total assorted	Cut 38 squares 4½″ × 4½″ for pieced border.	¼ yard total assorted	Cut 6 squares 4½″ × 4½″ for pieced border.
Reds	⅓ yard total assorted	Cut 3 each using appliqué pieces 1, 2, and 3. Cut 2 each using appliqué pieces 4, 5, and 6.	¼ yard total assorted	Cut 1 each using appliqué pieces 1, 2, and 3.
Golds, lights, pinks, and greens	½ yard total assorted	Cut 3 each using appliqué pieces 7 and 8; cut 2 each using appliqué pieces 9 and 10 (from golds). Cut 11 using appliqué piece 12 (from lights). Cut 11 using appliqué piece 13 (from pinks). Cut 9 using appliqué piece 14 (from greens).	¼ yard total assorted	Cut 1 each using appliqué pieces 7 and 8 (from golds). Cut 2 using appliqué piece 12 (from lights). Cut 2 using appliqué piece 13 (from pinks). Cut 3 using appliqué piece 14 (from greens).
Brown for runner	Scrap	Cut 2 using appliqué piece 11.		
Black	Scrap	Cut 5 using appliqué piece 15.	Scrap	Cut 1 using appliqué piece 15.
Backing and binding	2 yards		½ yard	
Batting	24″ × 68″		16″ × 24″	
Paper-backed fusible web	1½ yards		½ yard	

Bird Runner (20½″ × 64½″)

Place Mat (20½″ × 12½″)

Make the Runner and Place Mat

Refer to page 3 for general piecing and appliqué instructions.

1. Make the pieced background.

2. Fuse and stitch the appliqué pieces to the backgrounds and border squares.

3. Make the pieced borders and sew them to the runner / place mat top.

4. Layer, quilt, and bind the runner / place mat.

April

Made by Kim Schaefer
Quilted by Diane Minkley of Patched Works, Inc.

Raindrop Napkin

Materials and Cutting

Appliqué patterns are on pattern page P4. Refer to page 3 for preparing the appliqué.

MATERIALS	RUNNER		PLACE MAT	
Medium blues	⅔ yard total assorted	Cut 5 squares 10½″ × 10½″ for appliqué block backgrounds. Cut 11 using appliqué piece 14.	1 fat quarter	Cut 1 square 10½″ × 10½″ for appliqué block background. Cut 2 using appliqué piece 14.
Blue dot print	⅓ yard	Cut 6 rectangles 1½″ × 10½″ for lattice pieces and 2 strips 1½″ × 56½″ for side inner borders.	⅛ yard	Cut 2 rectangles 1½″ × 10½″ for side inner borders and 2 rectangles 1½″ × 12½″ for top and bottom inner borders.
Yellows, greens, blues, purples, reds, and oranges	1 yard total assorted	Cut 38 squares 4½″ × 4½″ for pieced border. Cut 5 each using appliqué pieces 2–5 (from yellows). Cut 5 each using appliqué pieces 6 and 7 (from greens). Cut 5 each using appliqué pieces 8–13 (from purples, reds, and oranges).	¼ yard total assorted	Cut 6 squares 4½″ × 4½″ for pieced border. Cut 1 each using appliqué pieces 2–5 (from yellows). Cut 1 each using appliqué pieces 6 and 7 (from greens). Cut 1 each using appliqué pieces 8–13 (from purples, reds, and oranges).
Black prints	⅓ yard total assorted	Cut 5 using appliqué piece 1.	¼ yard	Cut 1 using appliqué piece 1.
Backing and binding	2 yards		½ yard	
Batting	24″ × 68″		16″ × 24″	
Paper-backed fusible web	1½ yards		½ yard	

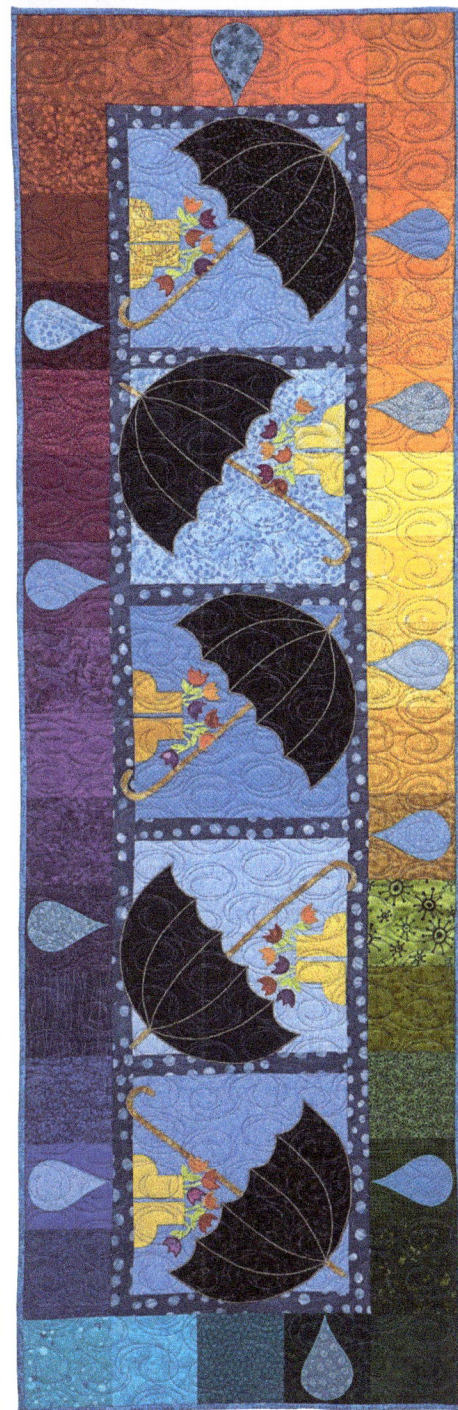

Umbrella Runner (20½″ × 64½″)

Place Mat (20½″ × 12½″)

Make the Runner and Place Mat

Refer to page 3 for general piecing and appliqué instructions. Refer to pattern page P4 for the numbers of the smaller appliqué pieces.

1. Make the pieced background.

2. Fuse and stitch the appliqué pieces to the backgrounds and border squares. I flipped the umbrella handle in 2 of the blocks for fun.

3. Make the pieced borders and sew them to the runner / place mat top.

4. Layer, quilt, and bind the runner / place mat.

May

Ladybug Napkin

Made by Kim Schaefer
Quilted by Diane Minkley of Patched Works, Inc.

Materials and Cutting

Appliqué patterns are on pattern page P5. Refer to page 3 for preparing the appliqué.

MATERIALS	RUNNER		PLACE MAT	
Lights	⅔ yard total assorted	Cut 5 squares 10½″ × 10½″ for appliqué block backgrounds.	1 fat quarter	Cut 1 square 10½″ × 10½″ for appliqué block background.
Green	⅓ yard	Cut 6 rectangles 1½″ × 10½″ for lattice pieces and 2 strips 1½″ × 54½″ for side inner borders.	⅛ yard	Cut 2 rectangles 1½″ × 10½″ for side inner borders and 2 rectangles 1½″ × 12½″ for top and bottom inner borders.
Greens	⅞ yard total assorted	Cut 38 squares 4½″ × 4½″ for pieced border. Cut 31 using appliqué piece 21.	¼ yard total assorted	Cut 6 squares 4½″ × 4½″ for pieced border. Cut 3 using appliqué piece 21.
Orange, purple, yellow, blue, and red	1 fat quarter each	Cut 1 each using appliqué piece 1.	1 fat quarter	Cut 1 using appliqué piece 1 (from purple).
Oranges, purples, yellows, blues, reds, and whites	⅓ yard total assorted	Cut 5 using appliqué piece 2; cut 3 each using appliqué pieces 5, 6, and 7 (from oranges, purples, yellows, blues, reds, and whites). Cut 2 each using appliqué pieces 8 (from reds), 14 and 15 (from whites), and 16 (from yellows).	⅛ yard total assorted	Cut 1 each using appliqué piece 2 (from purple) and pieces 5, 6, and 7 (from oranges and blue). Cut 1 each using appliqué pieces 8 (from red), 14 and 15 (from whites), and 16 (from yellow).
Black	¼ yard	Cut 5 using appliqué piece 3. Cut 3 using appliqué piece 4. Cut 2 each using appliqué pieces 9–13 and 17–20.	⅛ yard	Cut 1 each using appliqué pieces 3 and 4, 9–13, and 17–20.
Backing and binding	2 yards		½ yard	
Batting	24″ × 68″		16″ × 24″	
Paper-backed fusible web	2 yards		½ yard	

Flower Runner (20½″ × 64½″)

Make the Runner and Place Mat

Refer to page 3 for general piecing and appliqué instructions. Refer to pattern page P5 for the numbers of the smaller appliqué pieces.

1. Make the pieced background.

2. Fuse and stitch the appliqué pieces to the backgrounds and border squares.

3. Make the pieced borders and sew them to the runner / place mat top.

4. Layer, quilt, and bind the runner / place mat.

Place Mat (20½″ × 12½″)

June

Ant Napkin

Made by Kim Schaefer
Quilted by Diane Minkley of Patched Works, Inc.

Materials and Cutting

Appliqué patterns are on pattern page P6. Refer to page 3 for preparing the appliqué.

MATERIALS	RUNNER		PLACE MAT	
Lights	⅔ yard total assorted	Cut 5 squares 10½" × 10½" for appliqué block backgrounds.	1 fat quarter	Cut 1 square 10½" × 10½" for appliqué block background.
Green	⅓ yard	Cut 6 rectangles 1½" × 10½" for lattice pieces and 2 strips 1½" × 56½" for side inner borders.	⅛ yard	Cut 2 rectangles 1½" × 10½" for side inner borders and 2 rectangles 1½" × 12½" for top and bottom inner borders.
Greens	1¼ yards total assorted	Cut 38 squares 4½" × 4½" for pieced border. Cut 5 using appliqué piece 1. Cut 31 using appliqué piece 7.	¼ yard total assorted	Cut 6 squares 4½" × 4½" for pieced border. Cut 1 using appliqué piece 1. Cut 5 using appliqué piece 7.
Black	⅓ yard	Cut 2 using appliqué piece 5. Cut 25 using appliqué piece 4. Cut 7 using appliqué piece 6.	1 fat eighth	Cut 4 using appliqué piece 4. Cut 1 each using appliqué pieces 5 and 6.
White	⅓ yard	Cut 5 using appliqué piece 2.	6" × 10" rectangle	Cut 1 using appliqué piece 2.
Reds	½ yard total assorted	Cut 9 strips 1½" × width of fabric. Cut 5 using appliqué piece 3 (2 on dotted line) and 2 using appliqué piece 8.	⅛ yard total assorted	Cut 9 rectangles 1½" × 5½". Cut 1 each using appliqué pieces 3 (on dotted line) and 8.
Backing and binding	2 yards		½ yard	
Batting	24" × 68"		16" × 24"	
Paper-backed fusible web	1¾ yards		½ yard	

Make the Runner and Place Mat

Refer to page 3 for general piecing and appliqué instructions.

1. Arrange and sew together the 9 strips from the assorted reds for the watermelon. Press. Use for appliqué pieces 3 and 8.

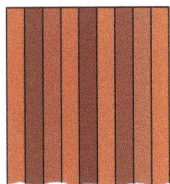

Sew strips.

2. Make the pieced background.

3. Fuse and stitch the appliqué pieces to the backgrounds and border squares.

4. Make the pieced borders and sew them to the runner / place mat top.

5. Layer, quilt, and bind the runner / place mat.

Watermelon Runner (20½" × 64½")

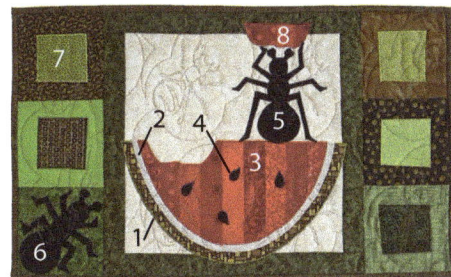

Place Mat (20½" × 12½")

July

Star Napkin

Made by Kim Schaefer
Quilted by Diane Minkley of Patched Works, Inc.

Materials and Cutting

Appliqué patterns are on pattern page P7. Refer to page 3 for preparing the appliqué.

MATERIALS	RUNNER		PLACE MAT	
Blues	⅔ yard total assorted	Cut 5 squares 10½″ × 10½″ for appliqué block backgrounds.	1 fat quarter	Cut 1 square 10½″ × 10½″ for appliqué block background.
Navy blue	⅓ yard	Cut 6 rectangles 1½″ × 10½″ for lattice pieces and 2 strips 1½″ × 56½″ for side inner borders.	⅛ yard	Cut 2 rectangles 1½″ × 10½″ for side inner borders and 2 rectangles 1½″ × 12½″ for top and bottom inner borders.
Lights	1⅛ yards total assorted	Cut 38 rectangles 2″ × 4½″ for pieced border. Cut 5 using appliqué piece 1.	⅜ yard total assorted	Cut 6 rectangles 2″ × 4½″ for pieced border. Cut 1 using appliqué piece 1.
Reds	¾ yard total assorted	Cut 76 rectangles 1¾″ × 4½″ for pieced border. Cut 5 using appliqué piece 2.	¼ yard total assorted	Cut 12 rectangles 1¾″ × 4½″ for pieced border. Cut 1 using appliqué piece 2.
Backing and binding	2 yards		½ yard	
Batting	24″ × 68″		16″ × 24″	
Paper-backed fusible web	1½ yards		½ yard	

Star Runner (20½″ × 64½″)

Place Mat (20½″ × 12½″)

Make the Runner and Place Mat

Refer to page 3 for general piecing and appliqué instructions.

1. Make the pieced background.

2. Piece the border blocks as shown. Make 38 blocks.

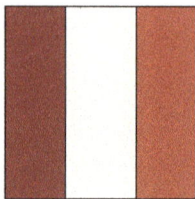

Make 38.

3. Arrange and sew together 2 rows of 14 blocks for each of the side borders. Press. Sew the 2 side borders to the runner. Press toward the border.

4. Arrange and sew together 2 rows of 5 blocks for each of the end borders. Press. Sew the 2 end borders to the runner. Press toward the borders.

5. Make 6 border blocks for the place mat. Arrange and sew together 2 rows of 3 blocks each. Sew to the sides of the place mat.

6. Fuse and stitch the appliqué pieces to the backgrounds.

7. Layer, quilt, and bind the runner.

August

Bee Napkin

Made by Kim Schaefer
Quilted by Diane Minkley of Patched Works, Inc.

Materials and Cutting

Appliqué patterns are on pattern page P8. Refer to page 3 for preparing the appliqué.

MATERIALS	RUNNER		PLACE MAT	
Lights	⅔ yard total assorted	Cut 5 squares 10½″ × 10½″ for appliqué block backgrounds.	1 fat quarter	Cut 1 square 10½″ × 10½″ for appliqué block background.
Tan	⅓ yard	Cut 6 rectangles 1½″ × 10½″ for lattice pieces and 2 strips 1½″ × 56½″ for side inner borders.	⅛ yard	Cut 2 rectangles 1½″ × 10½″ for side inner borders and 2 rectangles 1½″ × 12½″ for top and bottom inner borders.
Dark blues	⅔ yard total assorted	Cut 38 squares 4½″ × 4½″ for pieced border.	¼ yard total assorted	Cut 6 squares 4½″ × 4½″ for pieced border.
Medium and light blues	⅓ yard total	Cut 31 using appliqué piece 24.	⅛ yard total	Cut 4 using appliqué piece 24.
Golds	½ yard total assorted	Cut 5 each using appliqué pieces 1–9.	⅛ yard total assorted	Cut 1 each using appliqué pieces 1–9.
Black	⅛ yard	Cut 5 using appliqué piece 10. Cut 7 each using appliqué pieces 20–23.	⅛ yard	Cut 1 using appliqué piece 10. Cut 2 each using appliqué pieces 20–23.
Greens	⅓ yard total assorted	Cut 5 each using appliqué pieces 11 and 12.	⅛ yard total assorted	Cut 1 each using appliqué pieces 11 and 12.
Reds, oranges, purples, and teals	¼ yard total assorted	Cut 5 each using appliqué pieces 13–16.	⅛ yard total assorted	Cut 1 each using appliqué pieces 13–16 (from orange and purple).
Yellows	⅛ yard total assorted	Cut 7 using appliqué piece 17.	⅛ yard total assorted	Cut 2 using appliqué piece 17.
White	⅛ yard	Cut 7 each using appliqué pieces 18 and 19.	⅛ yard	Cut 2 each using appliqué pieces 18 and 19.
Backing and binding	2 yards		½ yard	
Batting	24″ × 68″		16″ × 24″	
Paper-backed fusible web	2¾ yards		½ yard	

Make the Runner and Place Mat

Refer to page 3 for general piecing and appliqué instructions. Refer to pattern page P8 for the numbers of the smaller appliqué pieces.

1. Make the pieced background.

2. Fuse and stitch the appliqué pieces to the backgrounds and border squares.

3. Make the pieced borders and sew them to the runner / place mat top.

4. Layer, quilt, and bind the runner / place mat.

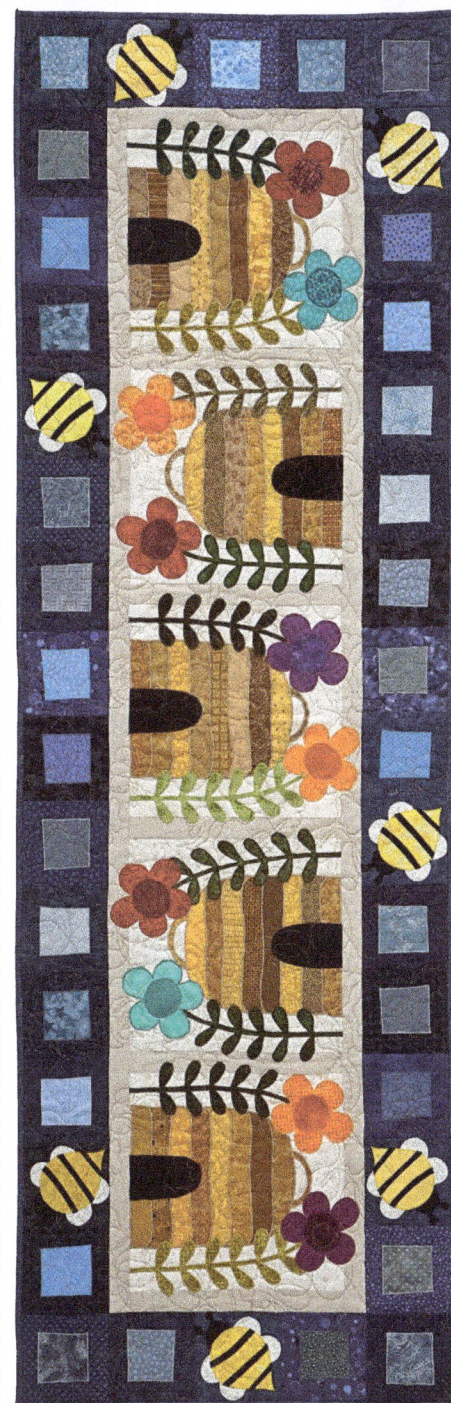

Bee Skep Runner (20½″ × 64½″)

Place Mat (20½″ × 12½″)

September

Made by Kim Schaefer
Quilted by Diane Minkley of Patched Works, Inc.

Apple Napkin

Materials and Cutting

Appliqué patterns are on pattern page P9. Refer to page 3 for preparing the appliqué.

MATERIALS	RUNNER		PLACE MAT	
Lights	1 yard total assorted	Cut 5 squares 10½″ × 10½″ for appliqué block backgrounds. Cut 5 each using appliqué pieces 3 and 4. Cut 1 each using appliqué pieces 8–13.	⅓ yard total assorted	Cut 1 square 10½″ × 10½″ for appliqué block background. Cut 1 each using appliqué pieces 3, 4, 8, 9, and 10.
Tan	⅓ yard	Cut 6 rectangles 1½″ × 10½″ for lattice pieces and 2 strips 1½″ × 56½″ for side inner borders.	⅛ yard	Cut 2 rectangles 1½″ × 10½″ for side inner borders and 2 rectangles 1½″ × 12½″ for top and bottom inner borders.
Golds, oranges, reds, greens, blues, and purples	⅔ yard total assorted	Cut 38 squares 4½″ × 4½″ for pieced border.	¼ yard total assorted	Cut 6 squares 4½″ × 4½″ for pieced border.
Reds	½ yard total assorted	Cut 5 using appliqué piece 1.	1 fat quarter	Cut 1 using appliqué piece 1.
Black	⅛ yard	Cut 5 using appliqué piece 2. Cut 30 using appliqué piece 5.	⅛ yard	Cut 1 using appliqué piece 2. Cut 6 using appliqué piece 5.
Greens	¼ yard total assorted	Cut 5 each using appliqué pieces 6 and 7.	Scraps	Cut 1 each using appliqué pieces 6 and 7.
Backing and binding	2 yards		½ yard	
Batting	24″ × 68″		16″ × 24″	
Paper-backed fusible web	1¾ yards		½ yard	

Apple Runner (20½″ × 64½″)

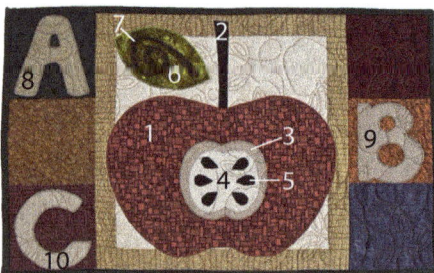

Place Mat (20½″ × 12½″)

Make the Runner and Place Mat

Refer to page 3 for general piecing and appliqué instructions.

1. Make the pieced background.

2. Fuse and stitch the appliqué pieces to the backgrounds and border squares.

3. Make the pieced borders and sew them to the runner / place mat top.

4. Layer, quilt, and bind the runner / place mat.

October

Made by Kim Schaefer
Quilted by Diane Minkley of Patched Works, Inc.

Candy Napkin

Materials and Cutting

Appliqué patterns are on pattern page P10. Refer to page 3 for preparing the appliqué.

MATERIALS	RUNNER		PLACE MAT	
Blacks	⅔ yard total assorted	Cut 5 squares 10½″ × 10½″ for appliqué block backgrounds.	1 fat quarter	Cut 1 square 10½″ × 10½″ for appliqué block background.
Black	⅔ yard	Cut 6 rectangles 1½″ × 10½″ for lattice pieces and 2 strips 1½″ × 56½″ for side inner borders. Cut 5 each using appliqué pieces 2 and 3. Cut 10 using appliqué piece 4.	¼ yard	Cut 2 rectangles 1½″ × 10½″ for side inner borders and 2 rectangles 1½″ × 12½″ for top and bottom inner borders. Cut 1 each using appliqué pieces 2 and 3. Cut 2 using appliqué piece 4.
Oranges and rusts	1½ yards total assorted	Cut 38 squares 4½″ × 4½″ for pieced border. Cut 5 using appliqué piece 1. Cut 8 using appliqué piece 7. Cut 30 using appliqué piece 9.	⅜ yard total assorted	Cut 6 squares 4½″ × 4½″ for pieced border. Cut 1 using appliqué piece 1. Cut 2 using appliqué piece 7. Cut 4 using appliqué piece 9.
Gold	⅛ yard	Cut 5 using appliqué piece 5.	Scrap	Cut 1 using appliqué piece 5.
White	⅛ yard	Cut 8 using appliqué piece 6.	Scrap	Cut 2 using appliqué piece 6.
Yellow	⅛ yard	Cut 8 using appliqué piece 8.	Scrap	Cut 2 using appliqué piece 8.
Backing and binding	2 yards		½ yard	
Batting	24″ × 68″		16″ × 24″	
Paper-backed fusible web	1½ yards		½ yard	

Make the Runner and Place Mat

Refer to page 3 for general piecing and appliqué instructions.

1. Make the pieced background.

2. Fuse and stitch the appliqué pieces to the backgrounds and border squares.

3. Make the pieced borders and sew them to the runner / place mat top.

4. Layer, quilt, and bind the runner / place mat.

Pumpkin Runner (20½″ × 64½″)

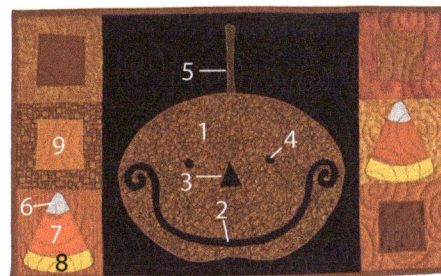

Place Mat (20½″ × 12½″)

November

Leaf Napkin

Made by Kim Schaefer
Quilted by Diane Minkley of Patched Works, Inc.

Materials and Cutting

Appliqué patterns are on pattern page P11. Refer to page 3 for preparing the appliqué.

MATERIALS	RUNNER		PLACE MAT	
Lights	⅔ yard total assorted	Cut 5 squares 10½″ × 10½″ for appliqué block backgrounds.	1 fat quarter	Cut 1 square 10½″ × 10½″ for appliqué block background.
Tan	⅓ yard	Cut 6 rectangles 1½″ × 10½″ for lattice pieces and 2 strips 1½″ × 56½″ for side inner borders.	⅛ yard	Cut 2 rectangles 1½″ × 10½″ for side inner borders and 2 rectangles 1½″ × 12½″ for top and bottom inner borders.
Golds	⅔ yard total assorted	Cut 38 squares 4½″ × 4½″ for pieced border.	¼ yard total assorted	Cut 6 squares 4½″ × 4½″ for pieced border.
Browns	½ yard total assorted	Cut 5 each using appliqué pieces 1 and 2.	¼ yard total assorted	Cut 1 each using appliqué pieces 1 and 2.
Reds, golds, oranges, rusts, and greens	¾ yard total assorted	Cut 5 using appliqué piece 3 (from reds). Cut 5 using appliqué piece 4 (from golds). Cut 5 using appliqué piece 5 (from oranges). Cut 5 each using appliqué pieces 6–11 (from reds, oranges, and rusts). Cut 2 using appliqué piece 12 (from green and rust). Cut 3 using appliqué piece 13 (from green, orange, and rust). Cut 1 using appliqué piece 14 (from rust). Cut 32 using appliqué piece 15.	¼ yard total assorted	Cut 1 using appliqué piece 3 (from red). Cut 1 using appliqué piece 4 (from gold). Cut 1 using appliqué piece 5 (from orange). Cut 1 each using appliqué pieces 6–11 (from reds, oranges, and rusts). Cut 1 each using appliqué pieces 12 and 14 (from rust and gold). Cut 4 using appliqué piece 15 (from gold, oranges, and green).
Backing and binding	2 yards		½ yard	
Batting	24″ × 68″		16″ × 24″	
Paper-backed fusible web	2 yards		½ yard	

Turkey Runner (20½″ × 64½″)

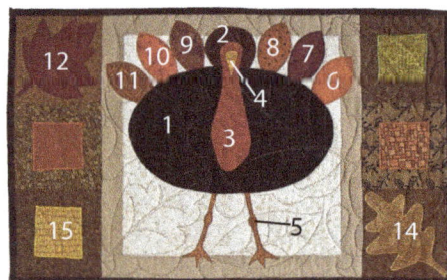
Place Mat (20½″ × 12½″)

Make the Runner and Place Mat

Refer to page 3 for general piecing and appliqué instructions.

1. Make the pieced background.

2. Fuse and stitch the appliqué pieces to the backgrounds and border squares.

3. Make the pieced borders and sew them to the runner / place mat top.

4. Layer, quilt, and bind the runner / place mat.

December

Made by Kim Schaefer
Quilted by Diane Minkley of Patched Works, Inc.

Present Napkin

Materials and Cutting

Appliqué patterns are on pattern page P12. Refer to page 3 for preparing the appliqué.

MATERIALS	RUNNER		PLACE MAT	
Tans	⅔ yard total assorted	Cut 5 squares 10½″ × 10½″ for appliqué block backgrounds.	1 fat quarter	Cut 1 square 10½″ × 10½″ for appliqué block background.
Green	⅓ yard	Cut 6 rectangles 1½″ × 10½″ for lattice pieces and 2 strips 1½″ × 56½″ for side inner borders.	⅛ yard	Cut 2 rectangles 1½″ × 10½″ for side inner borders and 2 rectangles 1½″ × 12½″ for top and bottom inner borders.
Reds	1 yard total assorted	Cut 38 squares 4½″ × 4½″ for pieced border. Cut 25 using appliqué piece 5. Cut 31 using appliqué piece 8.	¼ yard total assorted	Cut 6 squares 4½″ × 4½″ for pieced border. Cut 5 using appliqué piece 5. Cut 4 using appliqué piece 8.
Greens	½ yard total assorted	Cut 5 using appliqué piece 3. Cut 7 using appliqué piece 6.	¼ yard total assorted	Cut 1 using appliqué piece 3. Cut 2 using appliqué piece 6.
Lights	¼ yard total assorted	Cut 5 using appliqué piece 1. Cut 7 using appliqué piece 7.	Scraps	Cut 1 using appliqué piece 1. Cut 2 using appliqué piece 7.
Golds	Scraps	Cut 5 using appliqué piece 4.	Scrap	Cut 1 using appliqué piece 4.
Brown	Scrap	Cut 5 using appliqué piece 2.	Scrap	Cut 1 using appliqué piece 2.
Backing and binding	2 yards		½ yard	
Batting	24″ × 68″		16″ × 24″	
Paper-backed fusible web	1¾ yards		½ yard	

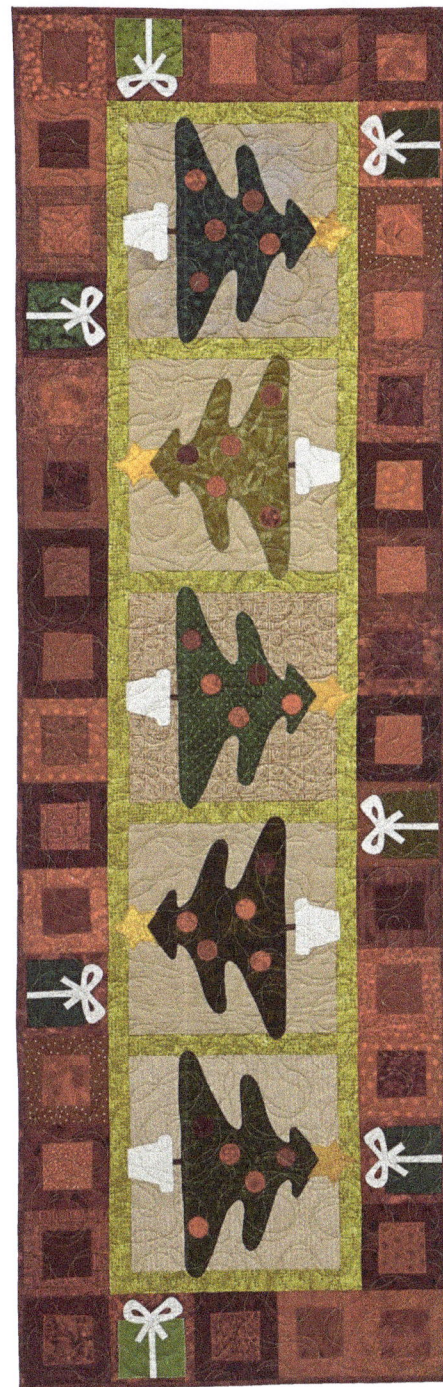

Make the Runner and Place Mat

Refer to page 3 for general piecing and appliqué instructions.

1. Make the pieced background.

2. Fuse and stitch the appliqué pieces to the backgrounds and border squares.

3. Make the pieced borders and sew them to the runner / place mat top.

4. Layer, quilt, and bind the runner / place mat.

Tree Runner (20½″ × 64½″)

Place Mat (20½″ × 12½″)

January

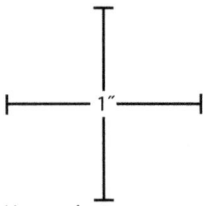

Use a ruler to measure these inch marks to verify that printout is correctly sized.

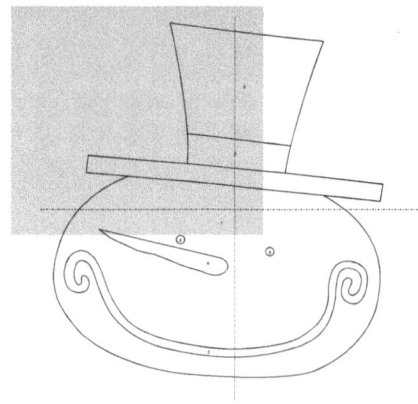

To make complete pattern, join the following pages, following the diagram for reference.

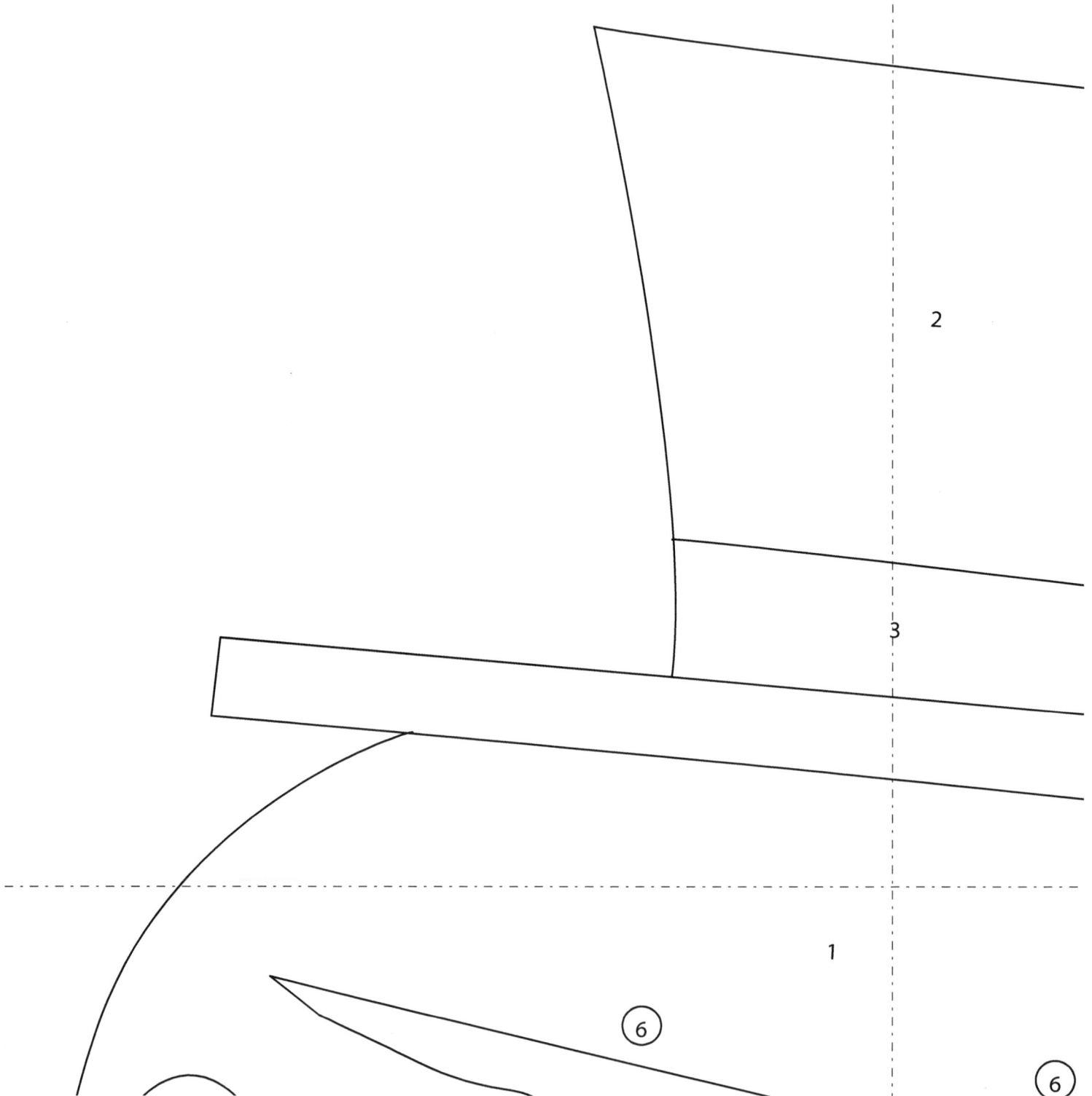

2

3

1

⑥

⑥

January

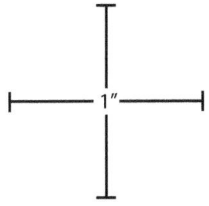

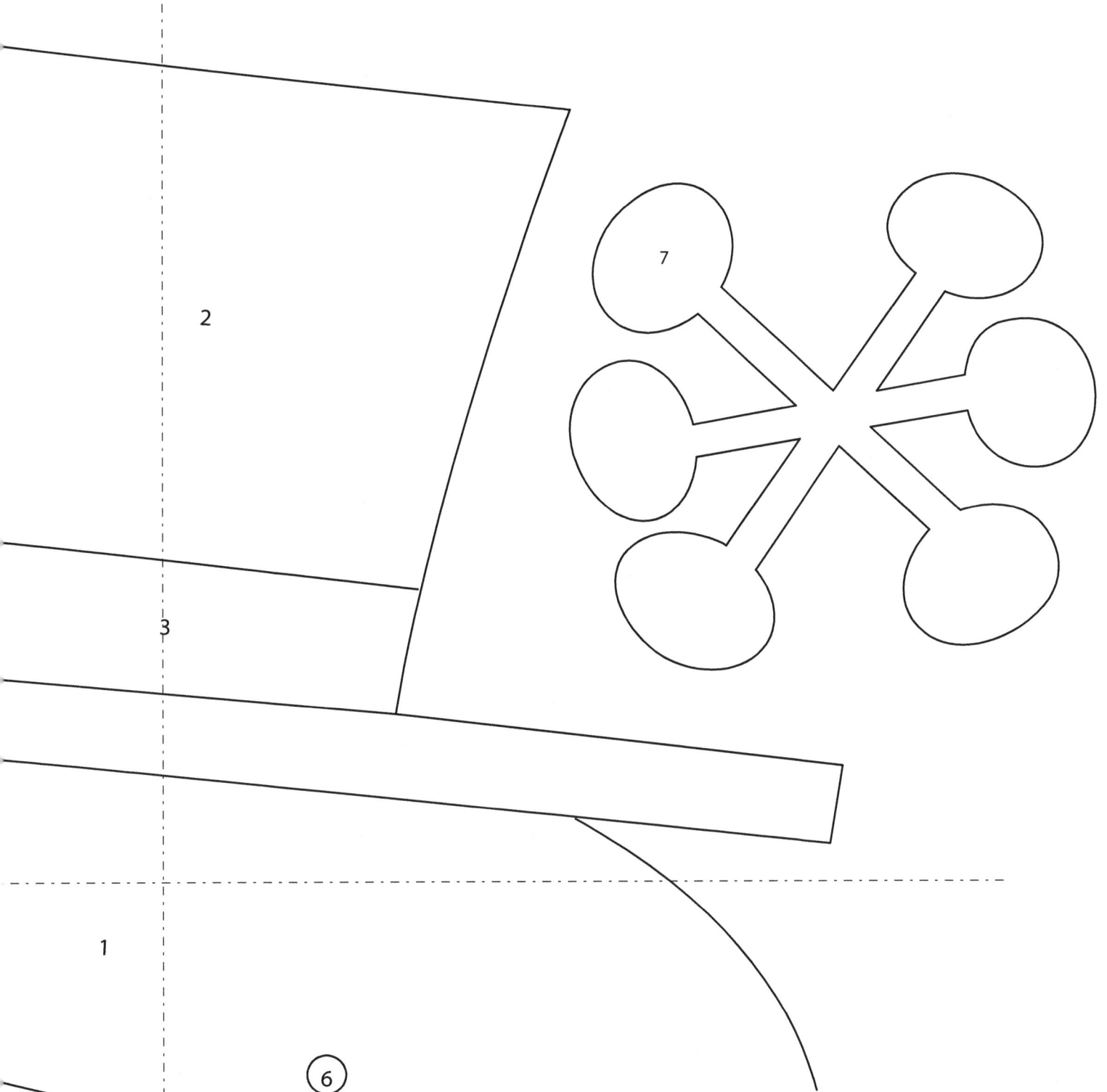

2

3

1

7

January

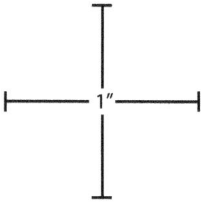

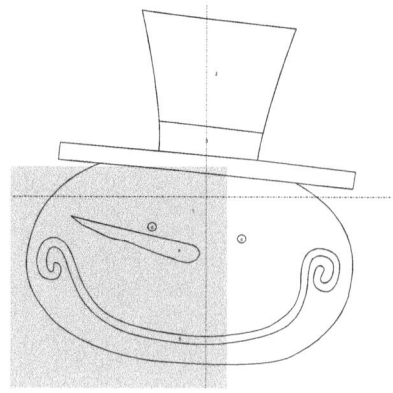

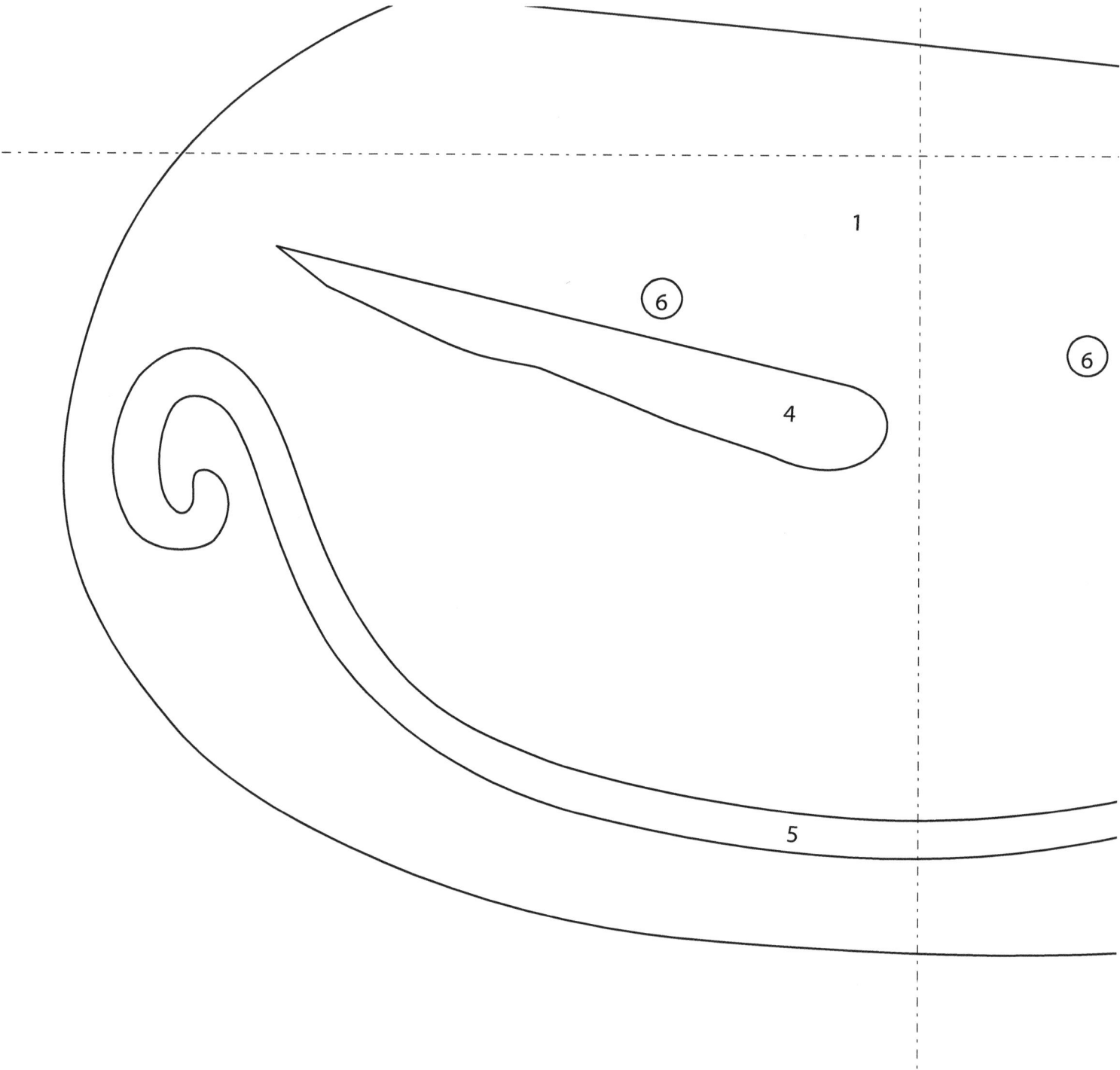

1

6

6

4

5

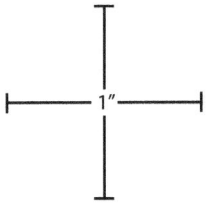

1"

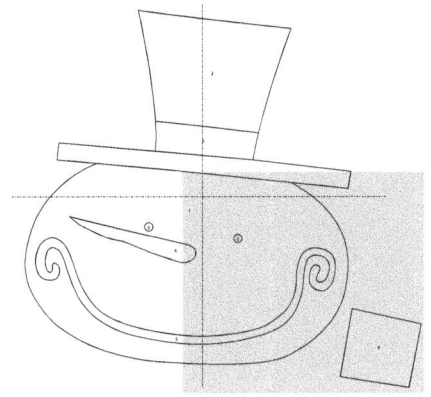

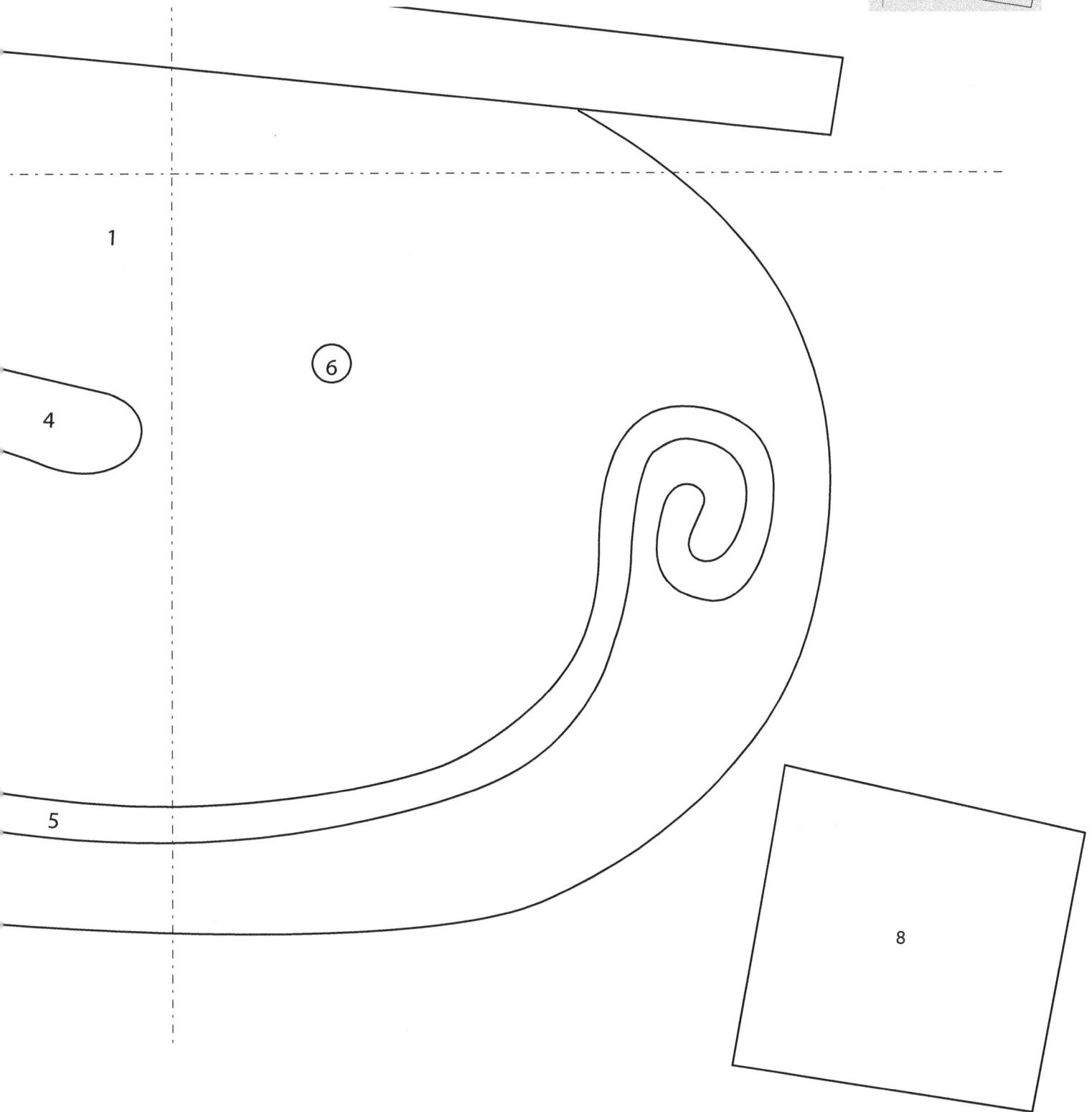

1

6

4

5

8

February

1"

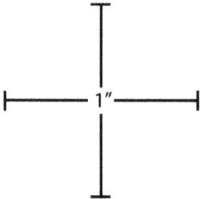

To make complete pattern, join the following
pages, following the diagram for reference.

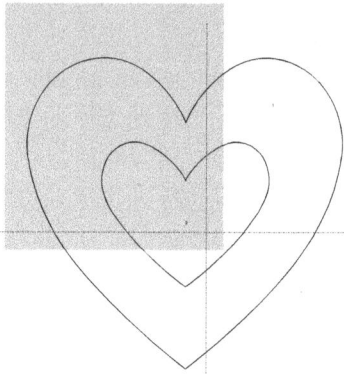

2

February

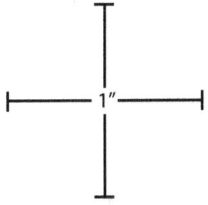

1

2

February

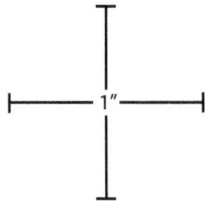

1"

2

3

February

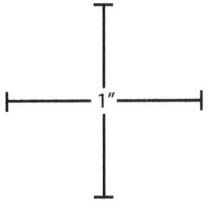

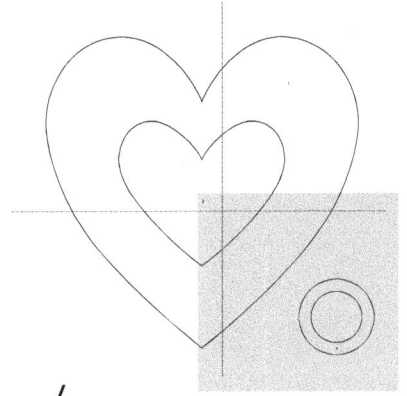

2

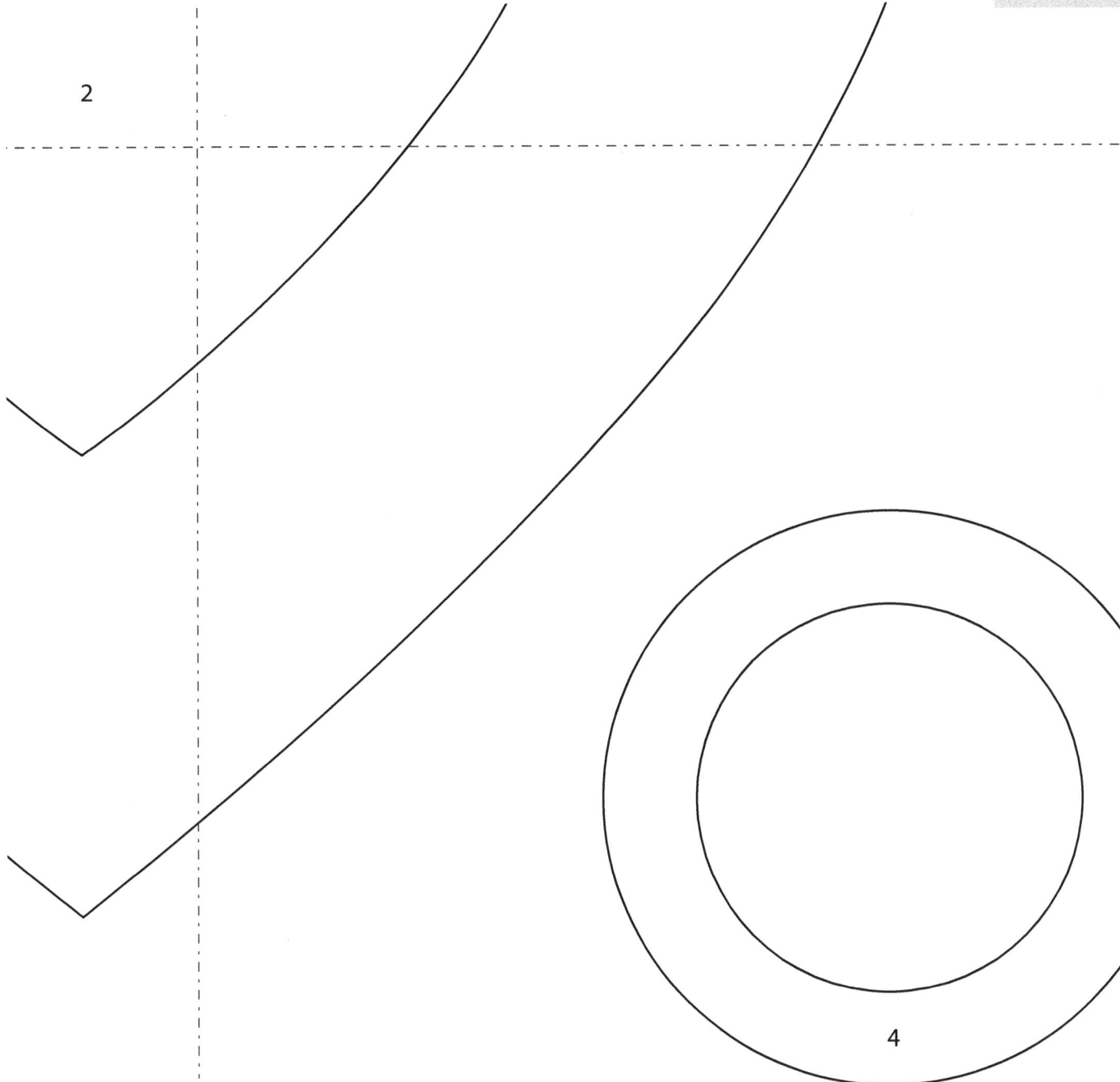

4

February

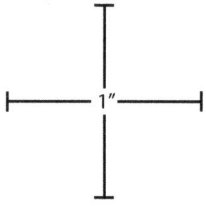

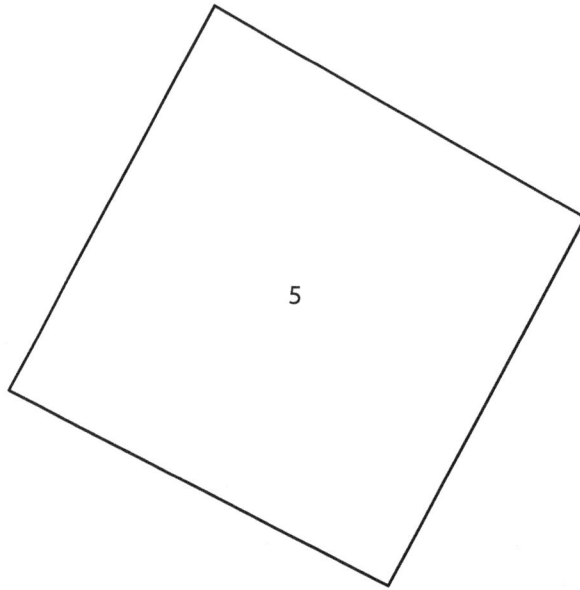

5

Napkin

March

1"

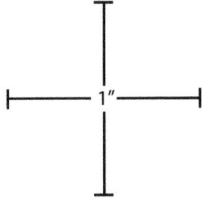

To make complete pattern, join the following pages, following the diagram for reference.

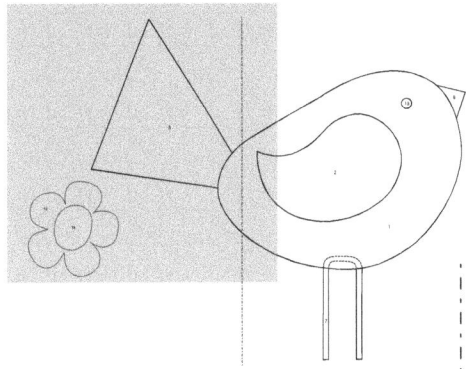

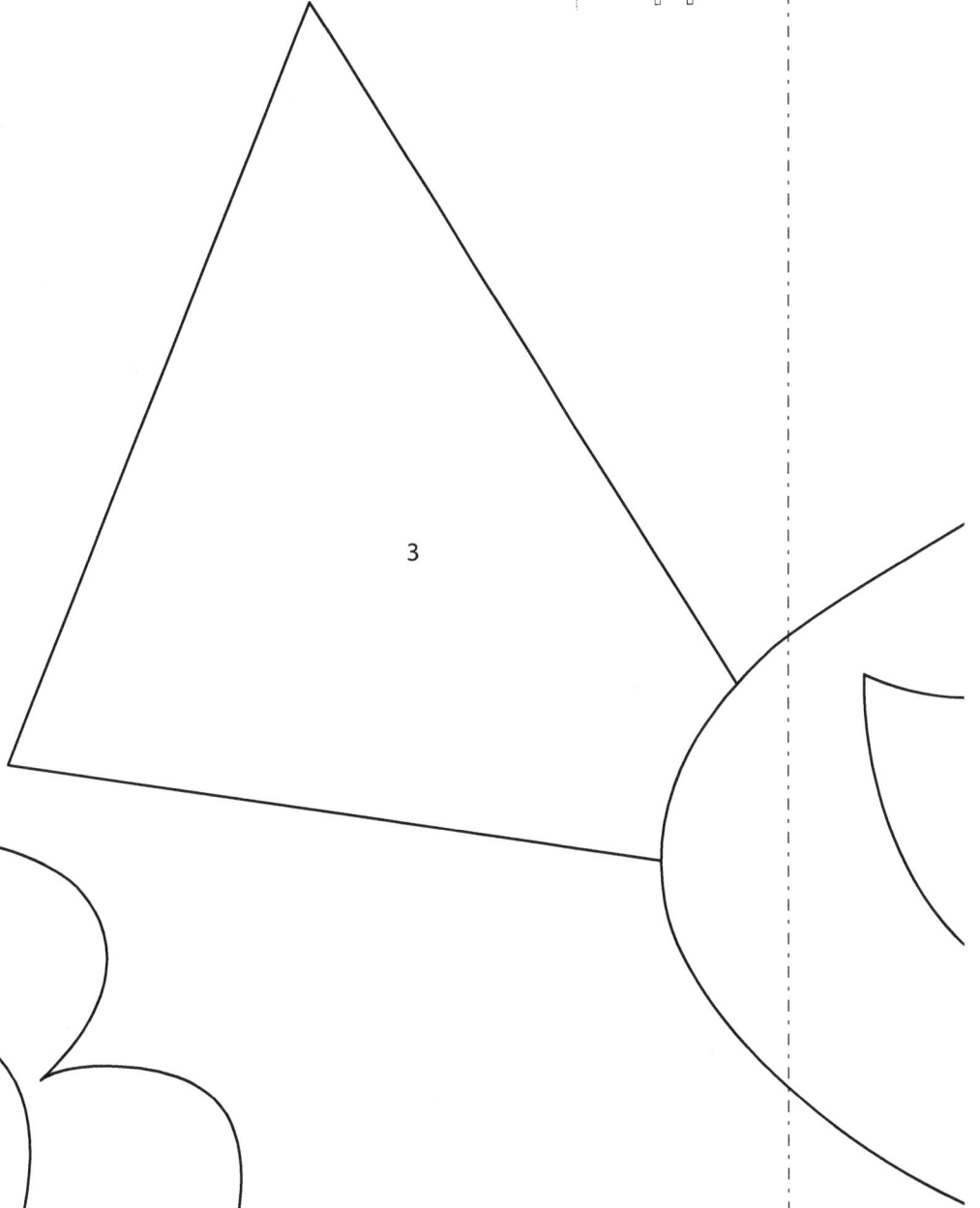

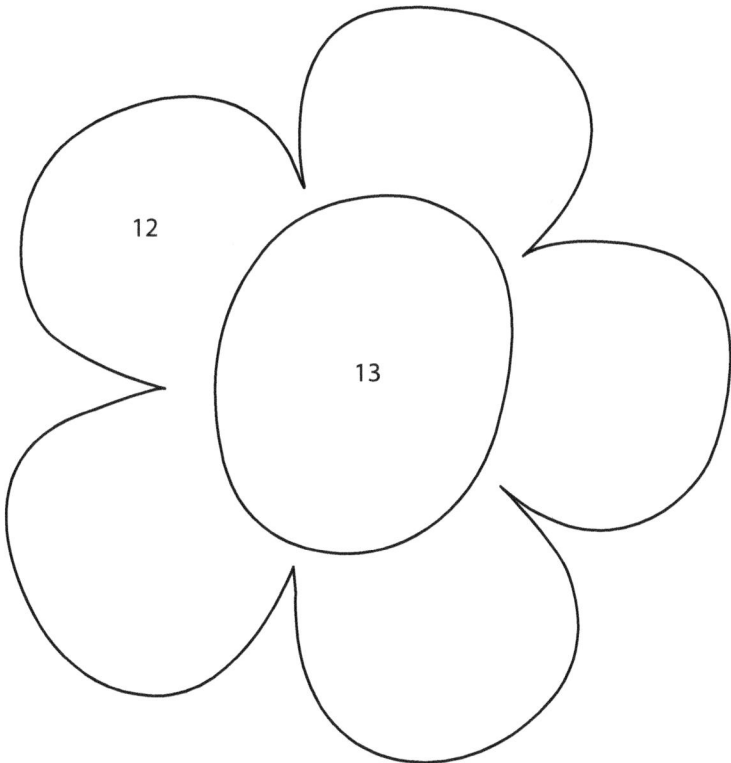

3

12

13

March

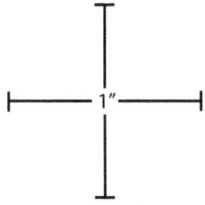

1"

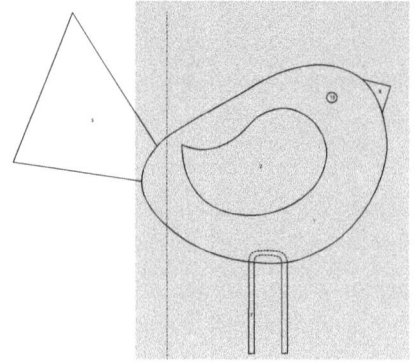

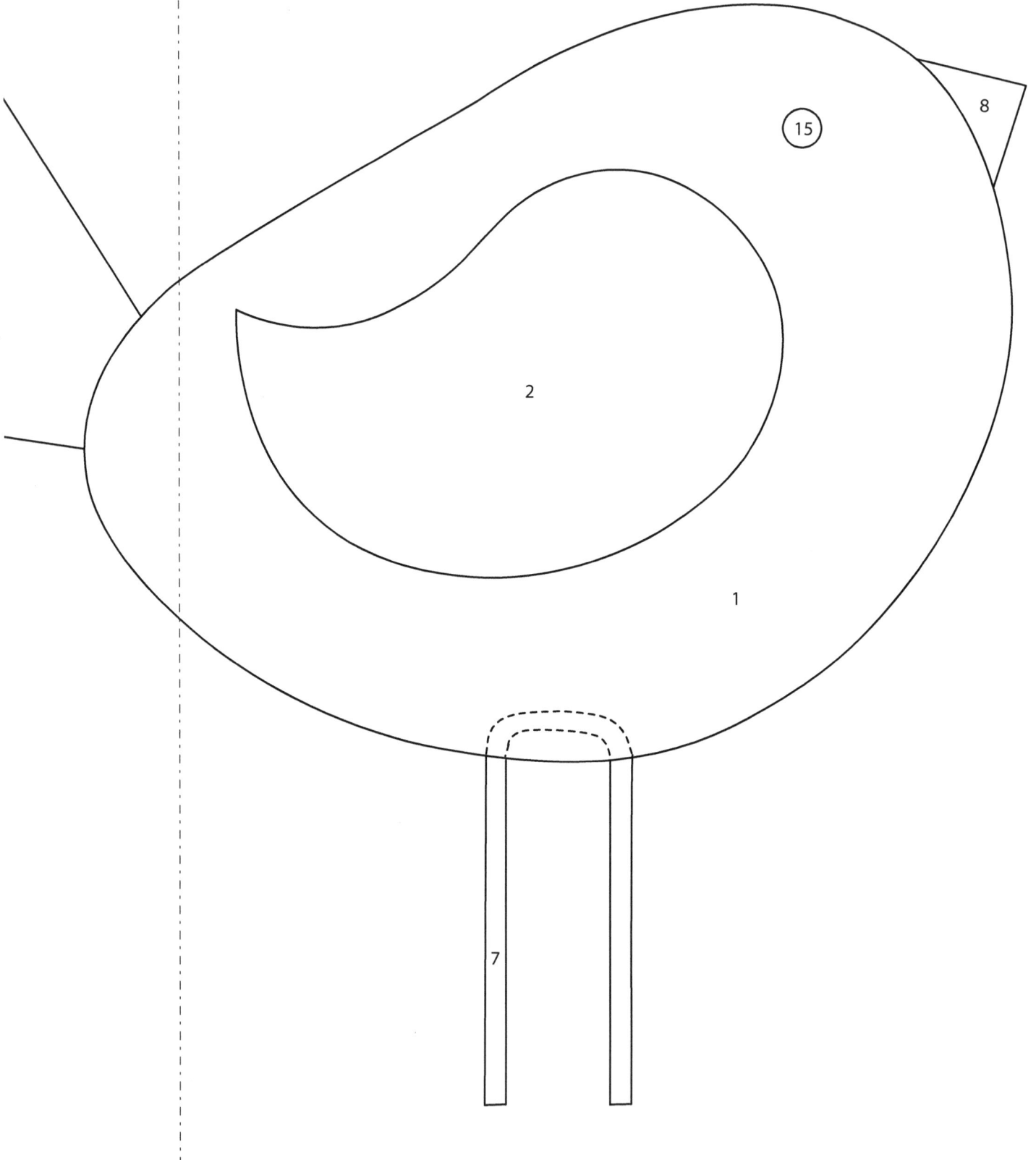

15

8

2

1

7

March

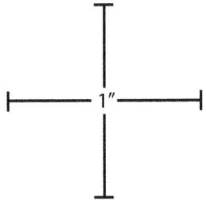

To make complete pattern, join the following
pages, following the diagram for reference.

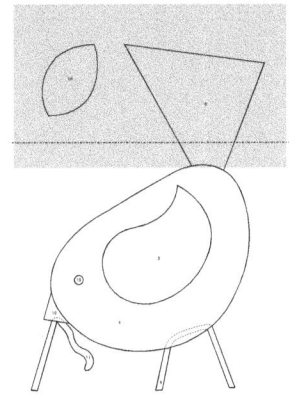

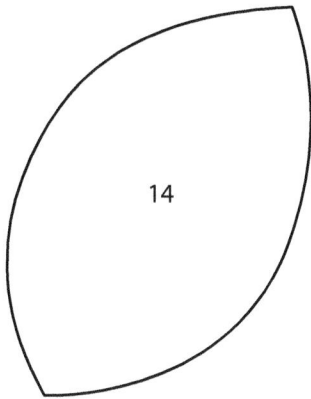

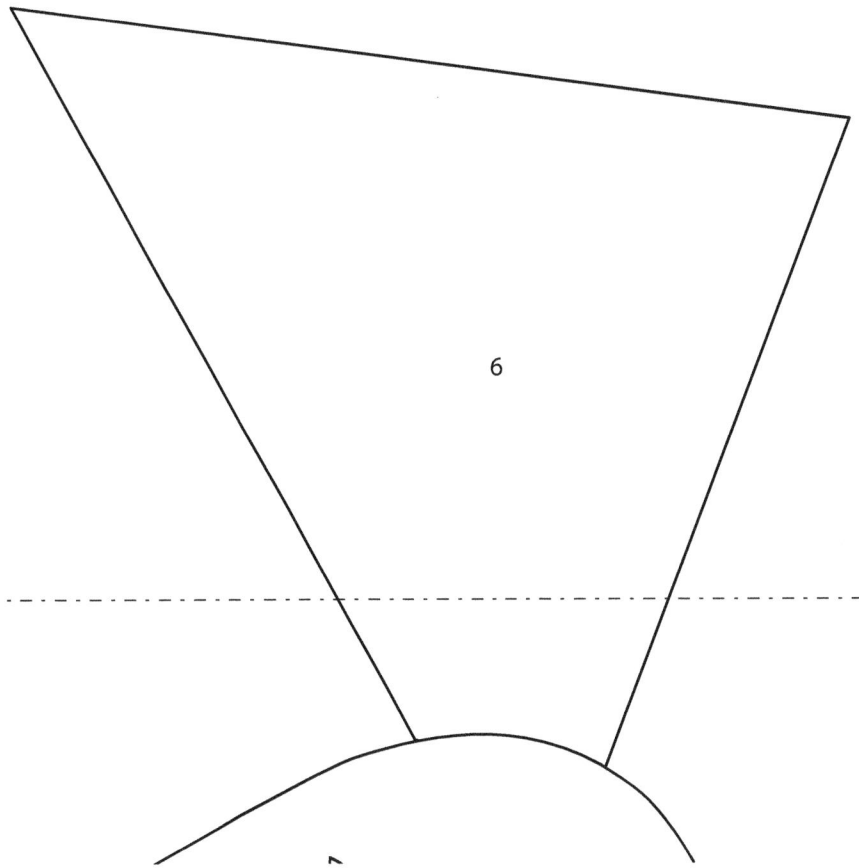

14

6

March

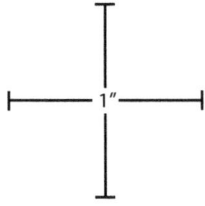

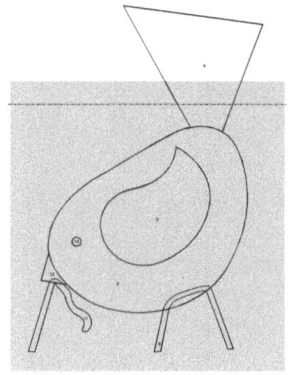

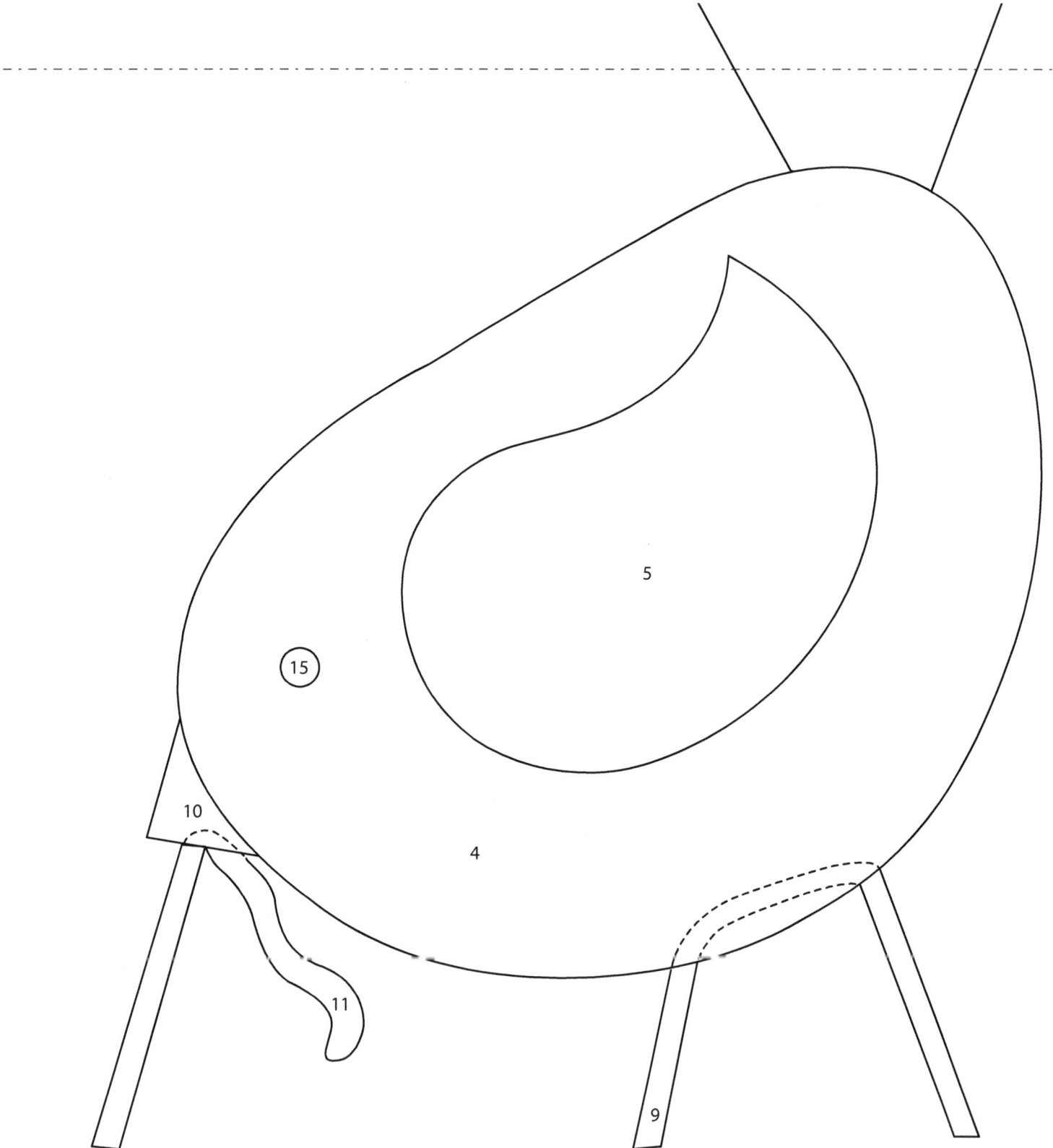

15

5

10

4

11

9

April

1"

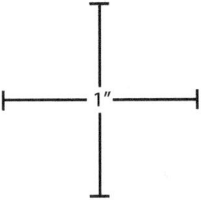

To make complete pattern, join the following
pages, following the diagram for reference.

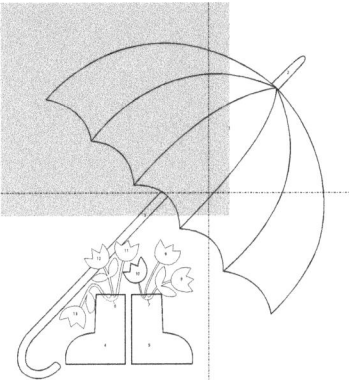

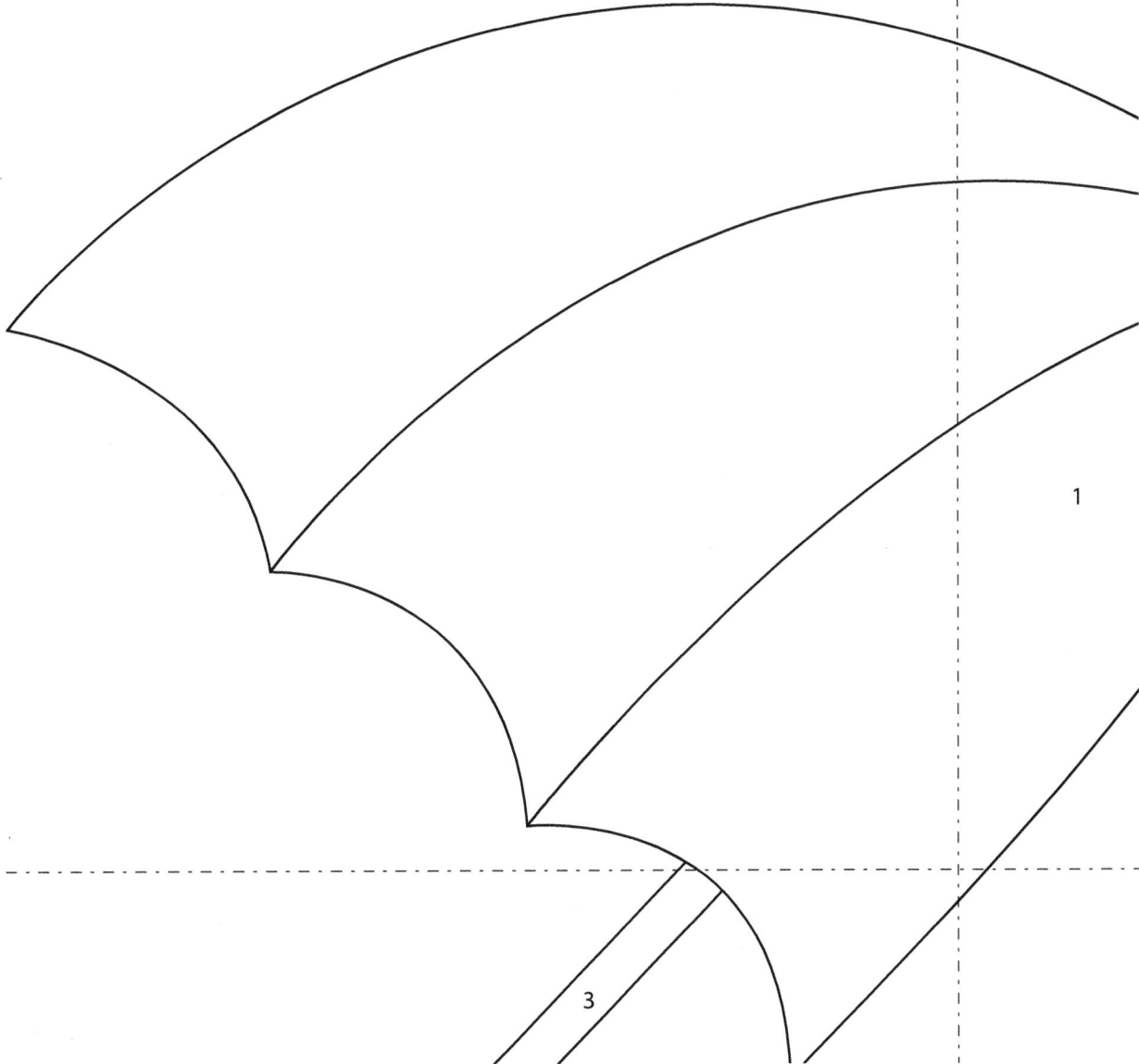

1

3

April

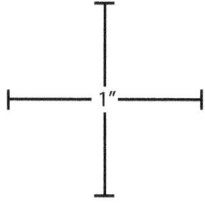

1"

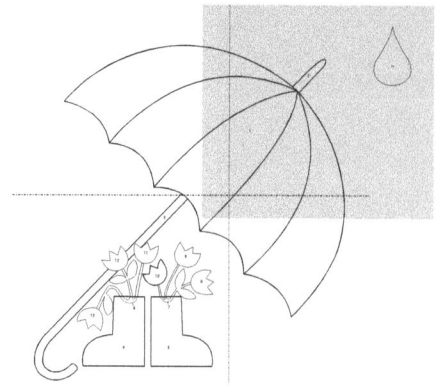

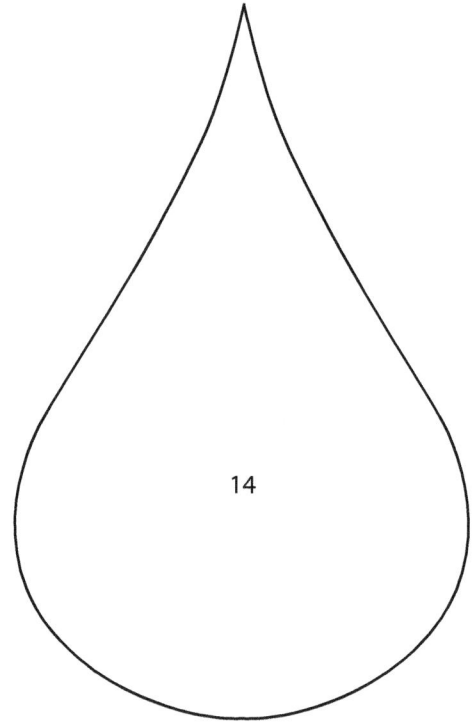

14

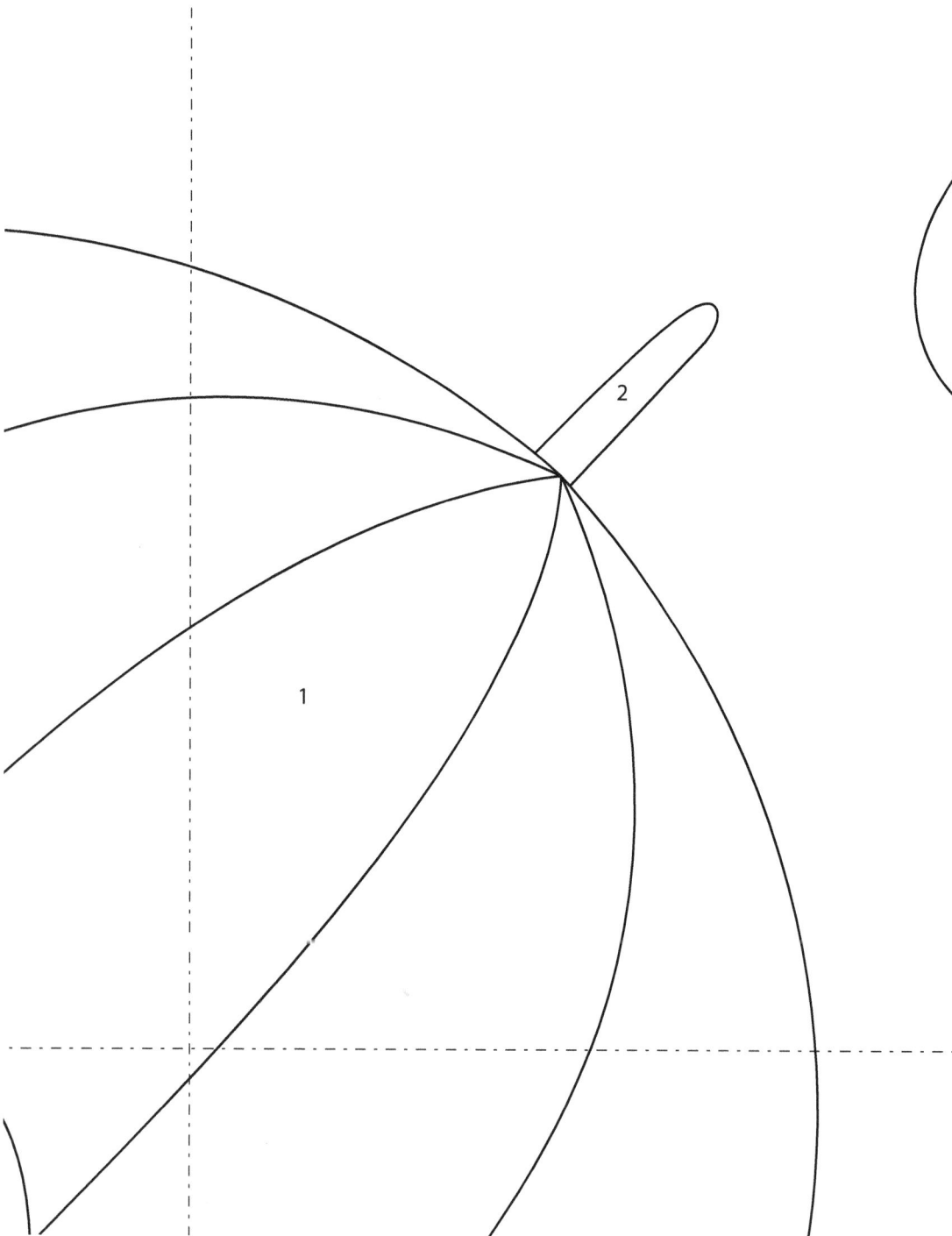

2

1

April

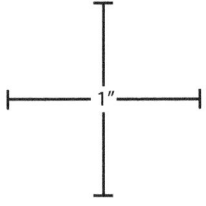

1"

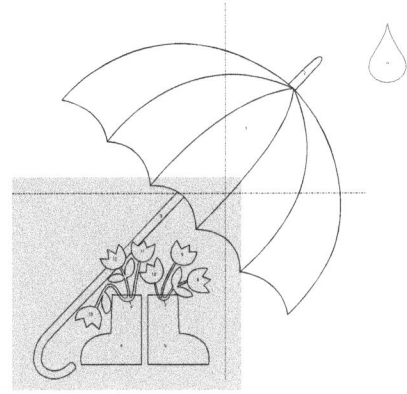

April

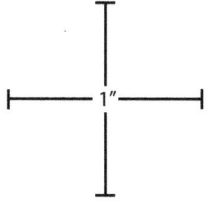

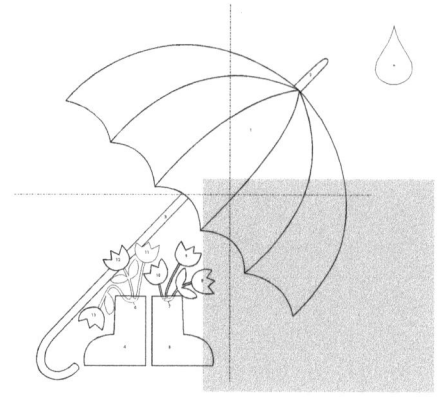

8

May

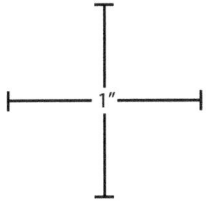

To make complete pattern, join the following pages, following the diagram for reference.

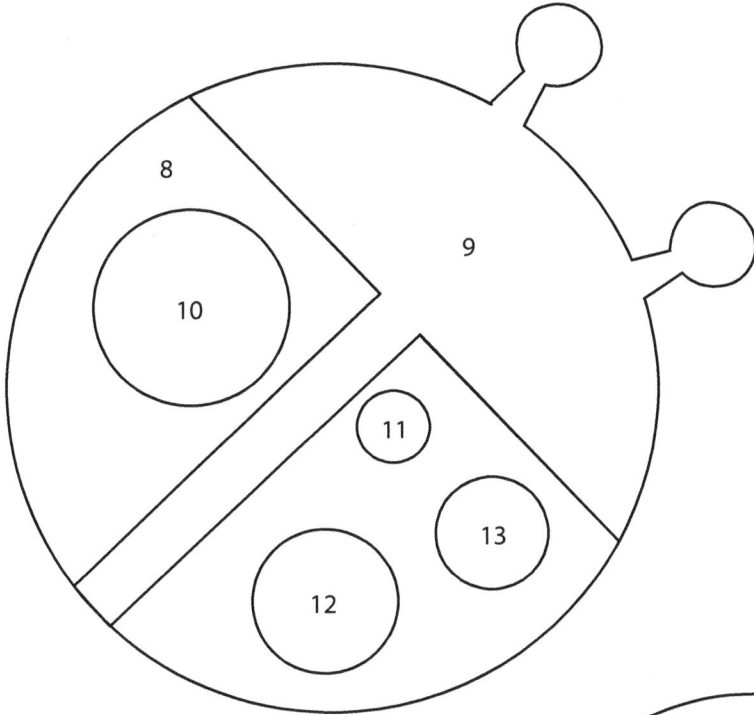

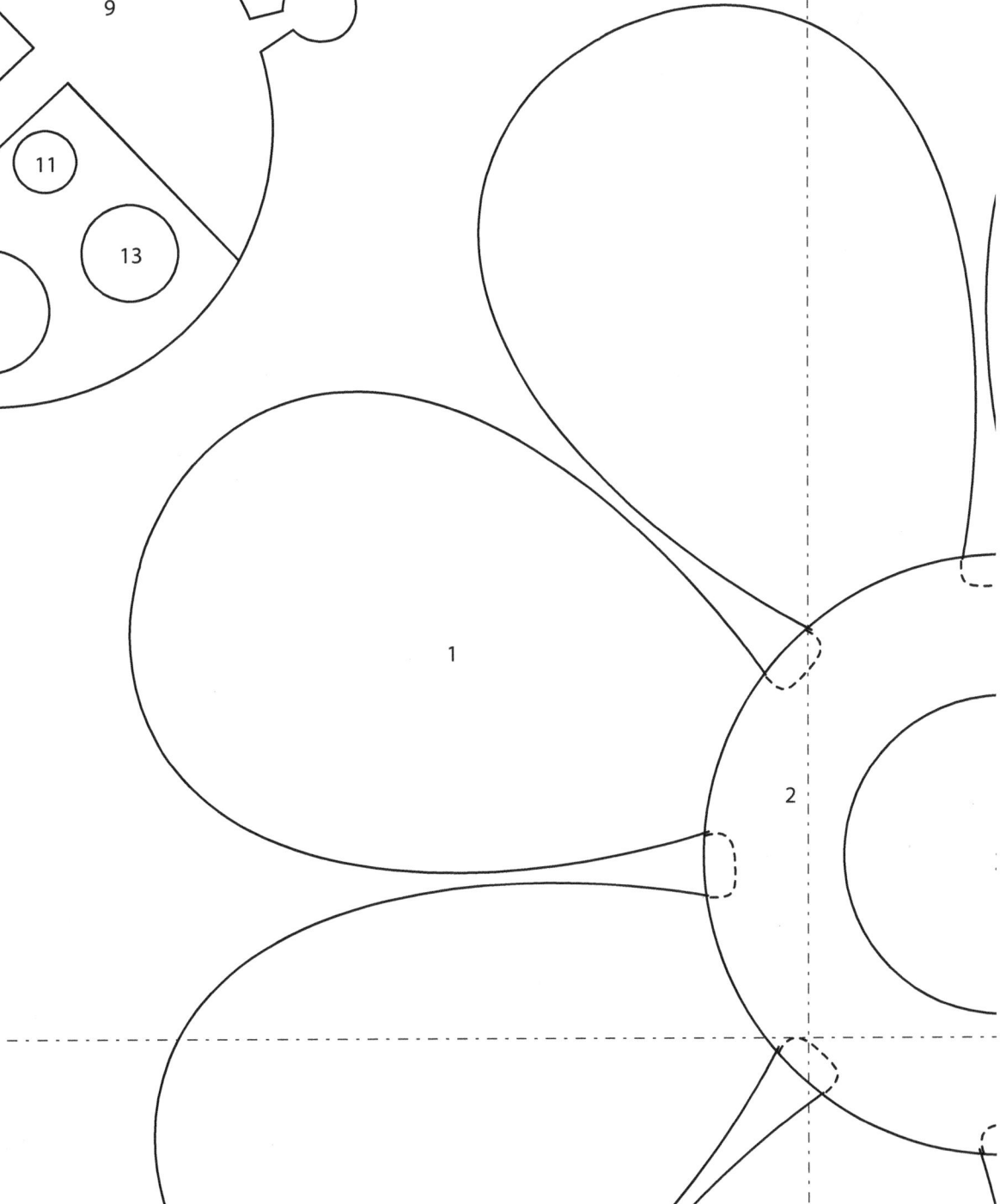

1"

8

9

10

11

13

12

1

2

May

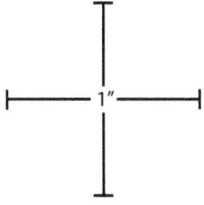

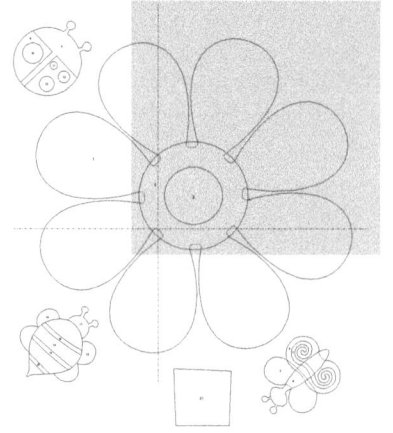

2

3

May

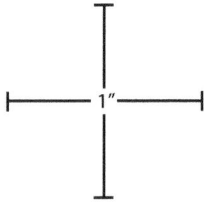

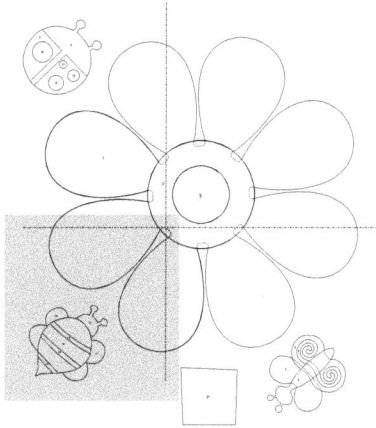

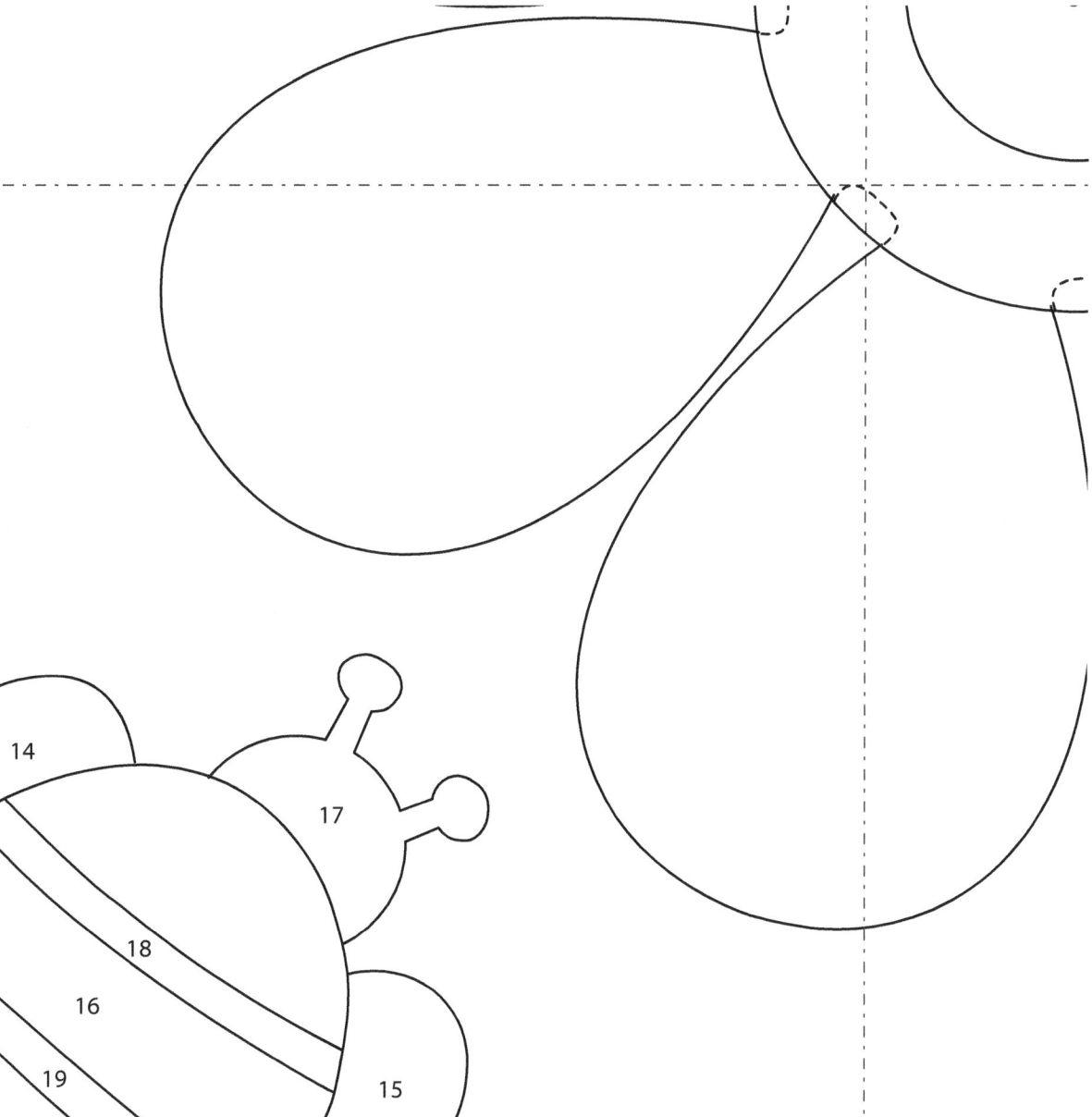

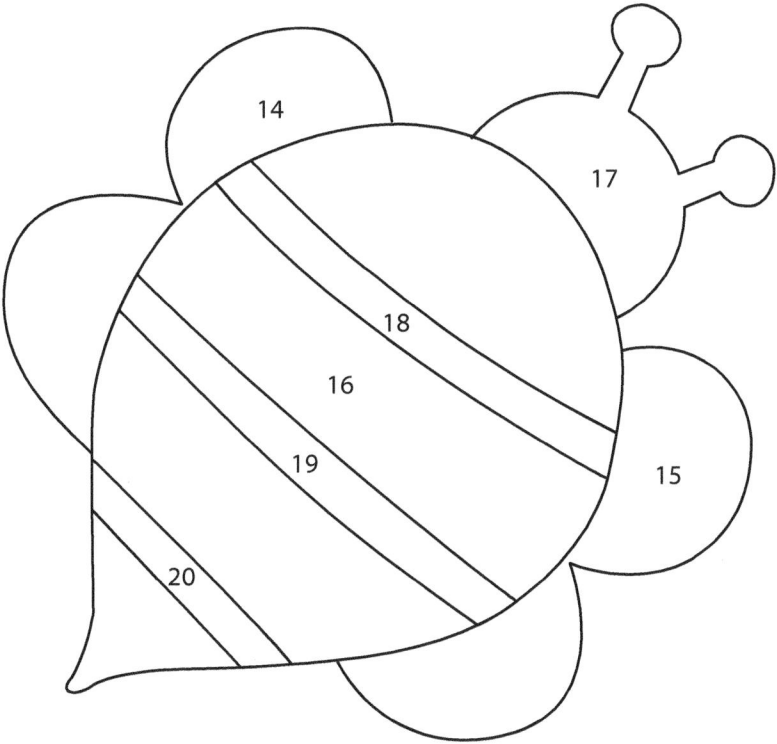

14

17

18

16

19

15

20

May

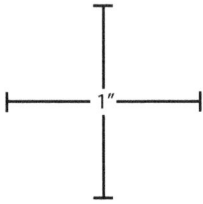

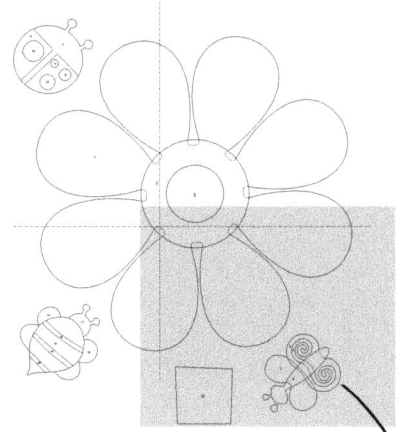

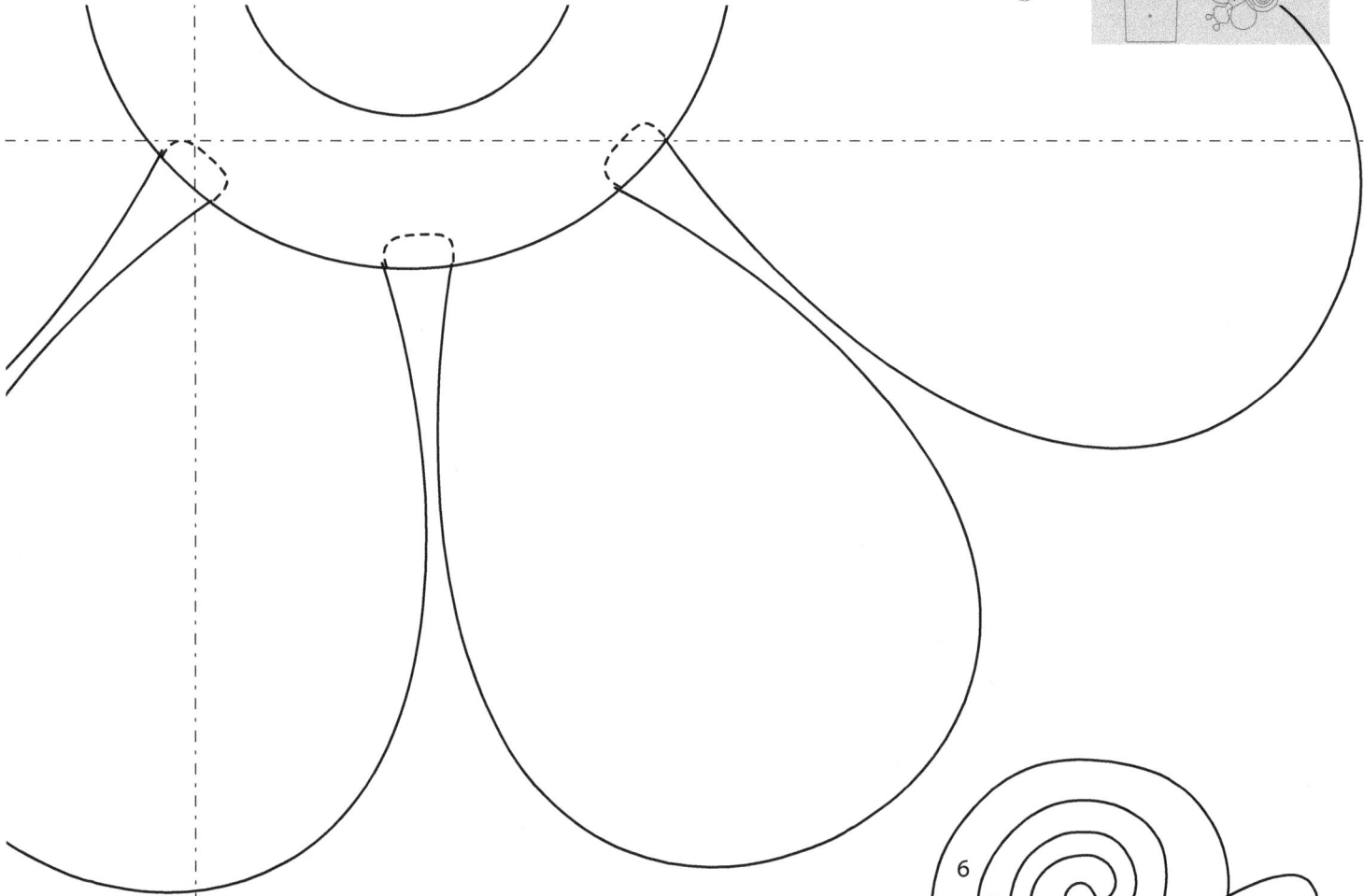

21

6
7

5

4

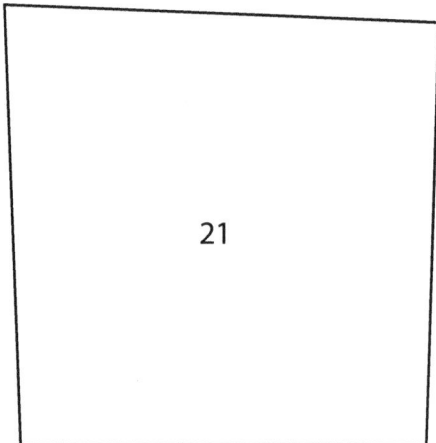

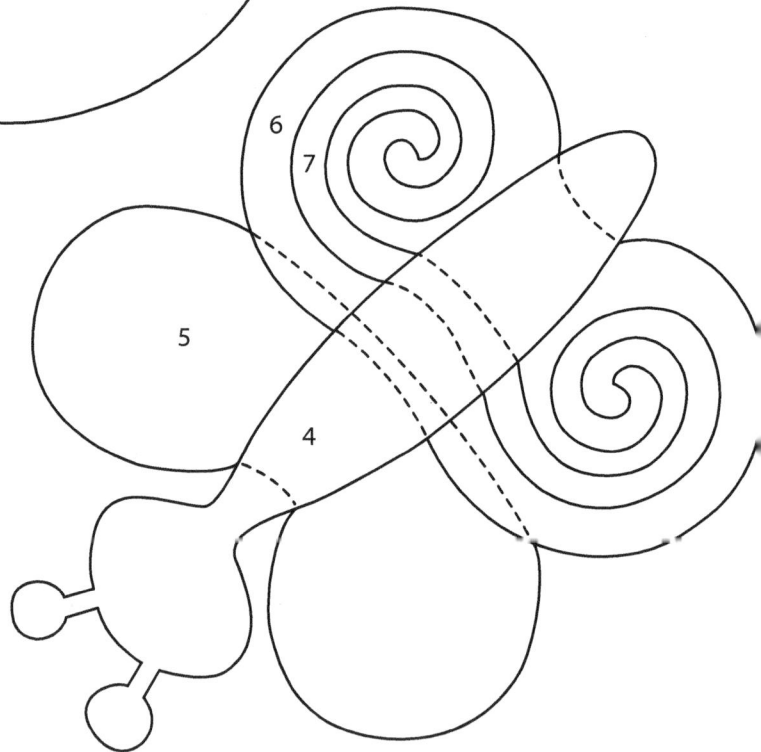

June

1"

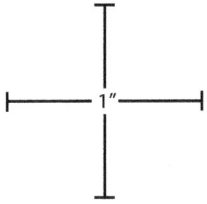

To make complete pattern, join the following
pages, following the diagram for reference.

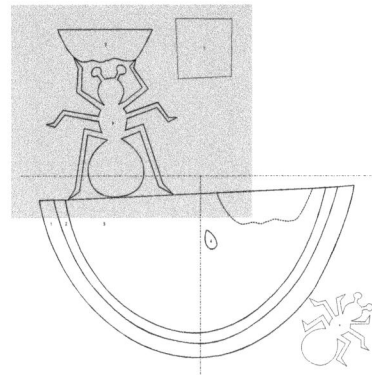

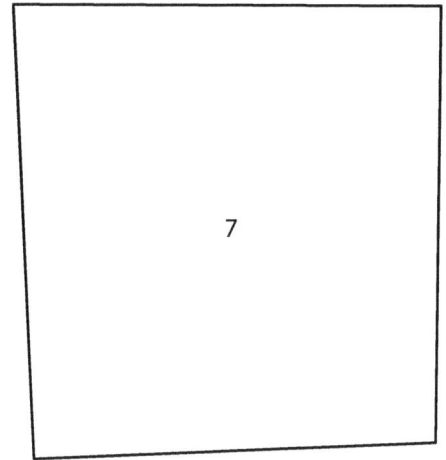

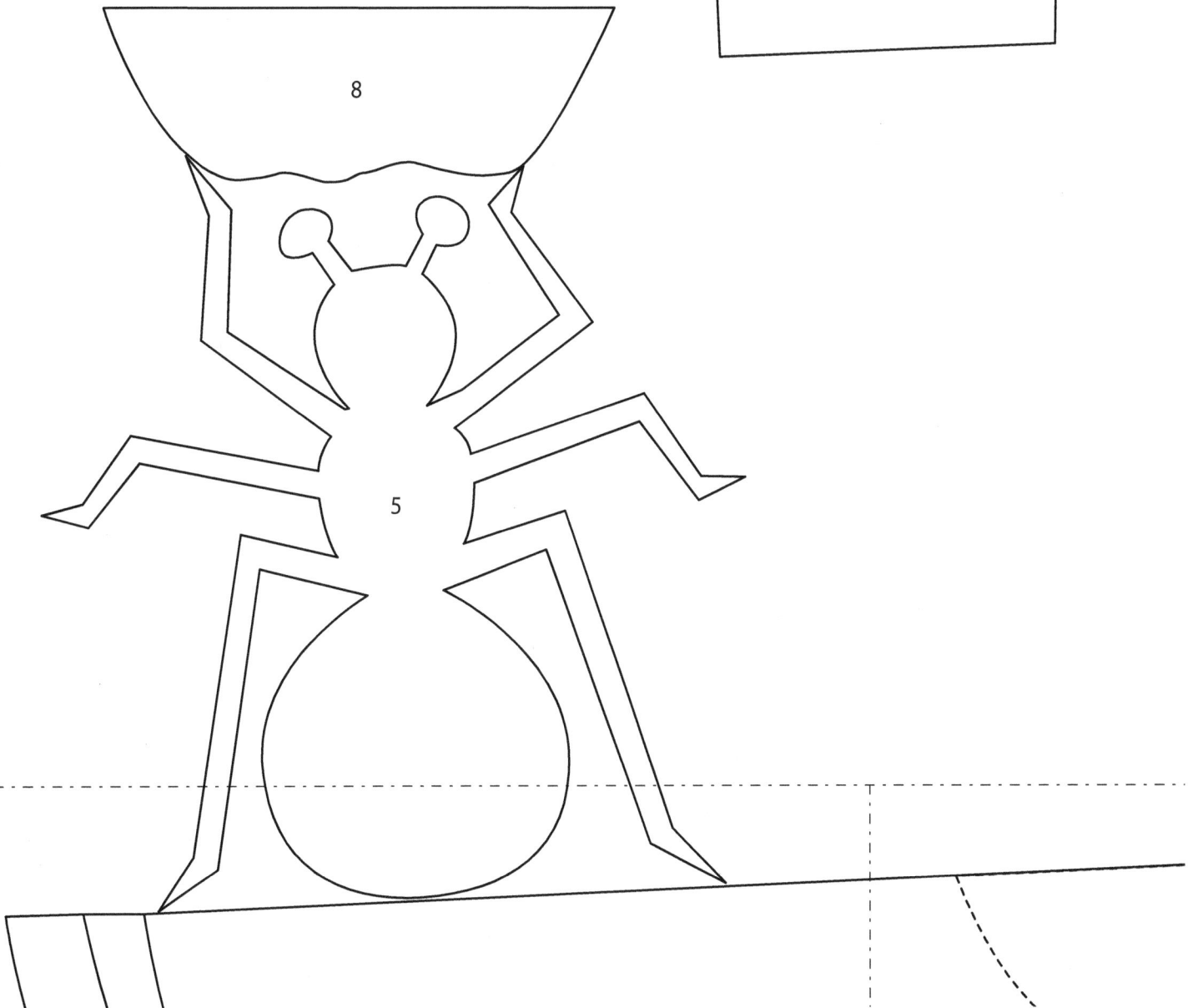

7

8

5

June

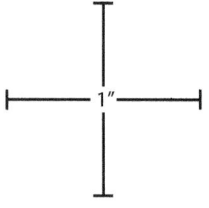

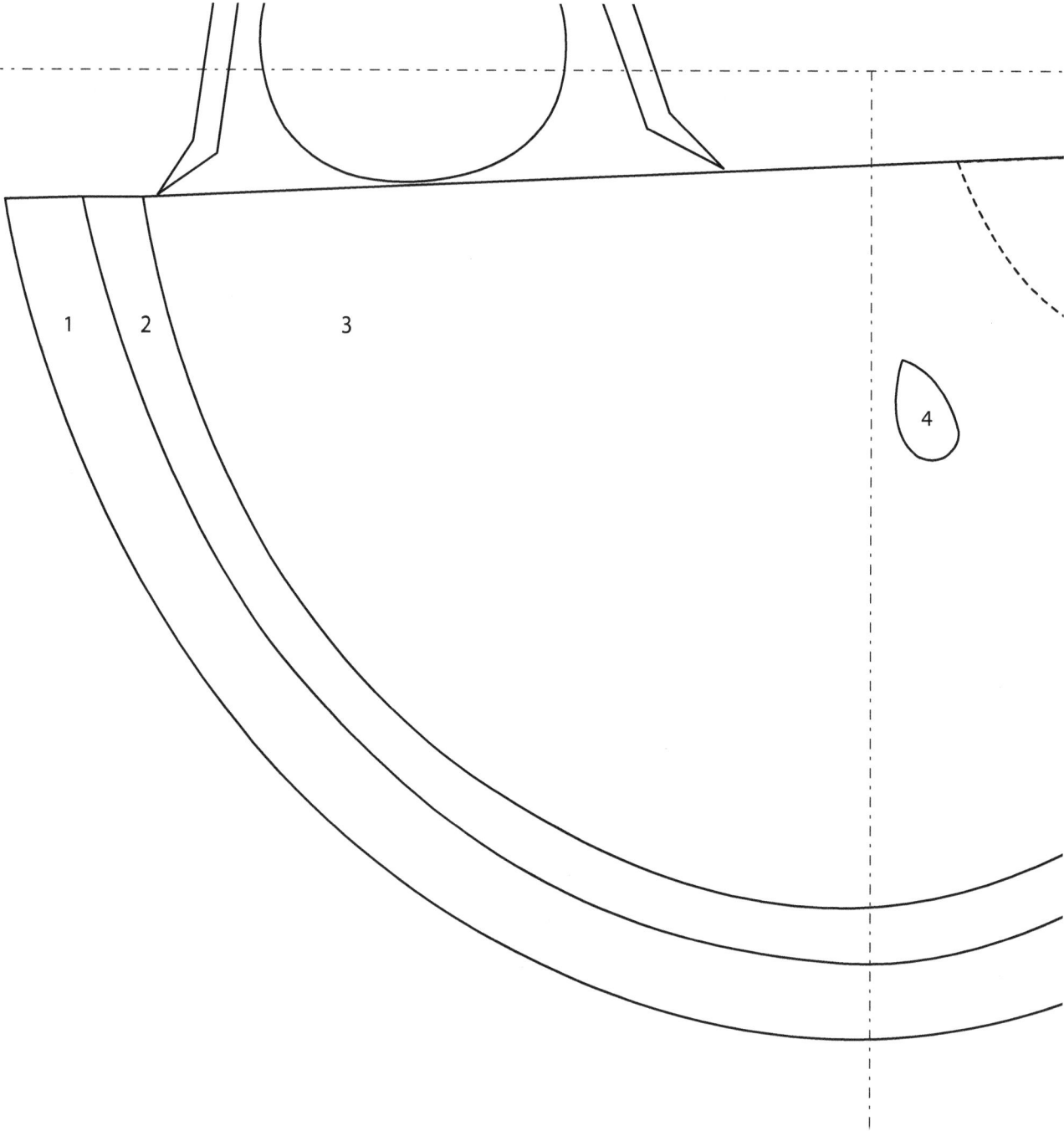

1

2

3

4

June

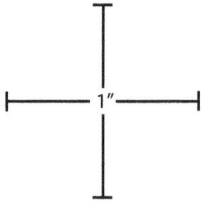

4

6

July

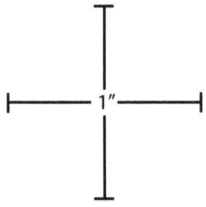

To make complete pattern, join the following
pages, following the diagram for reference.

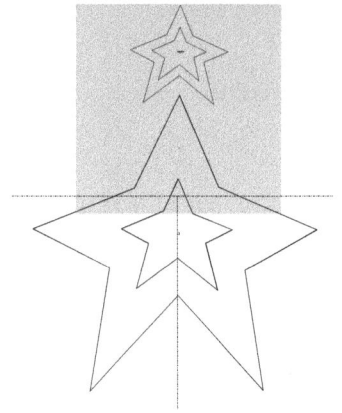

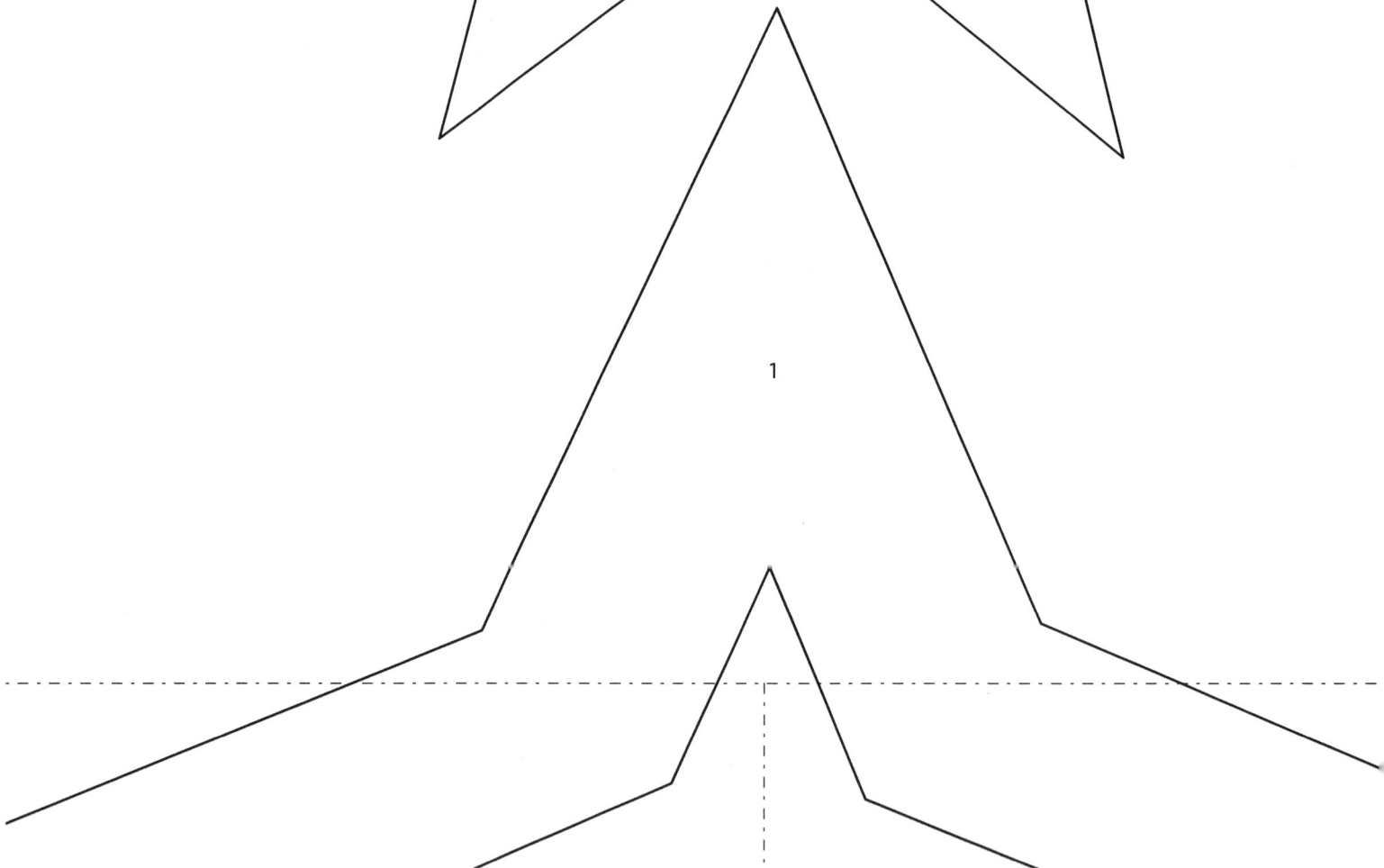

1"

Napkin

1

July

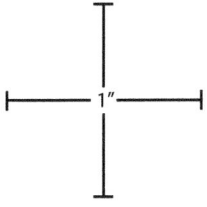

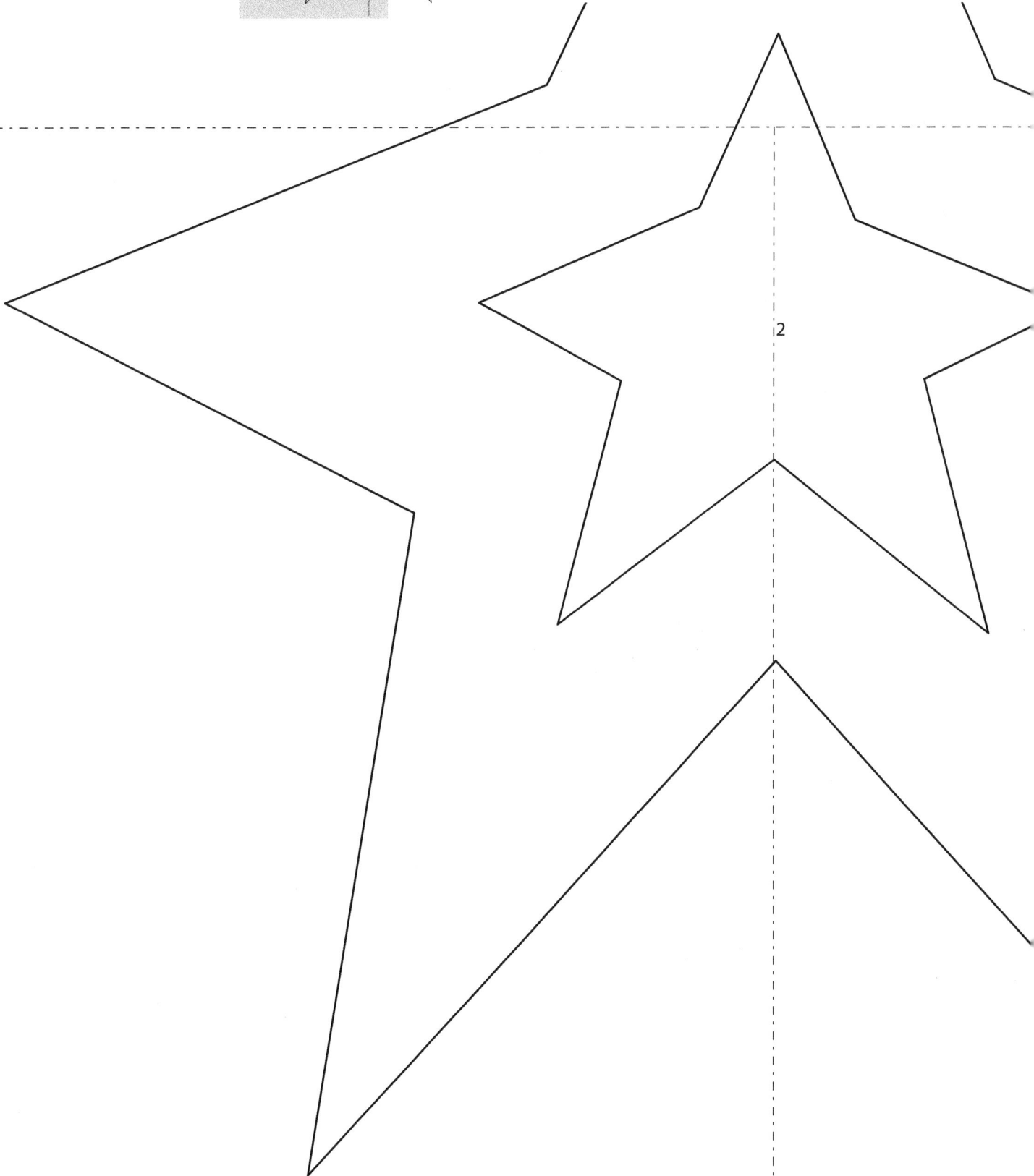

2

July

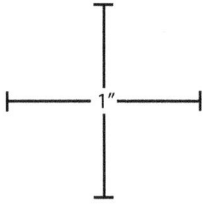

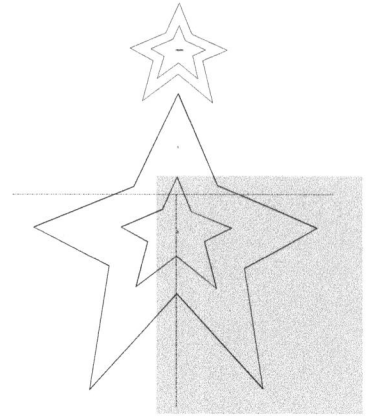

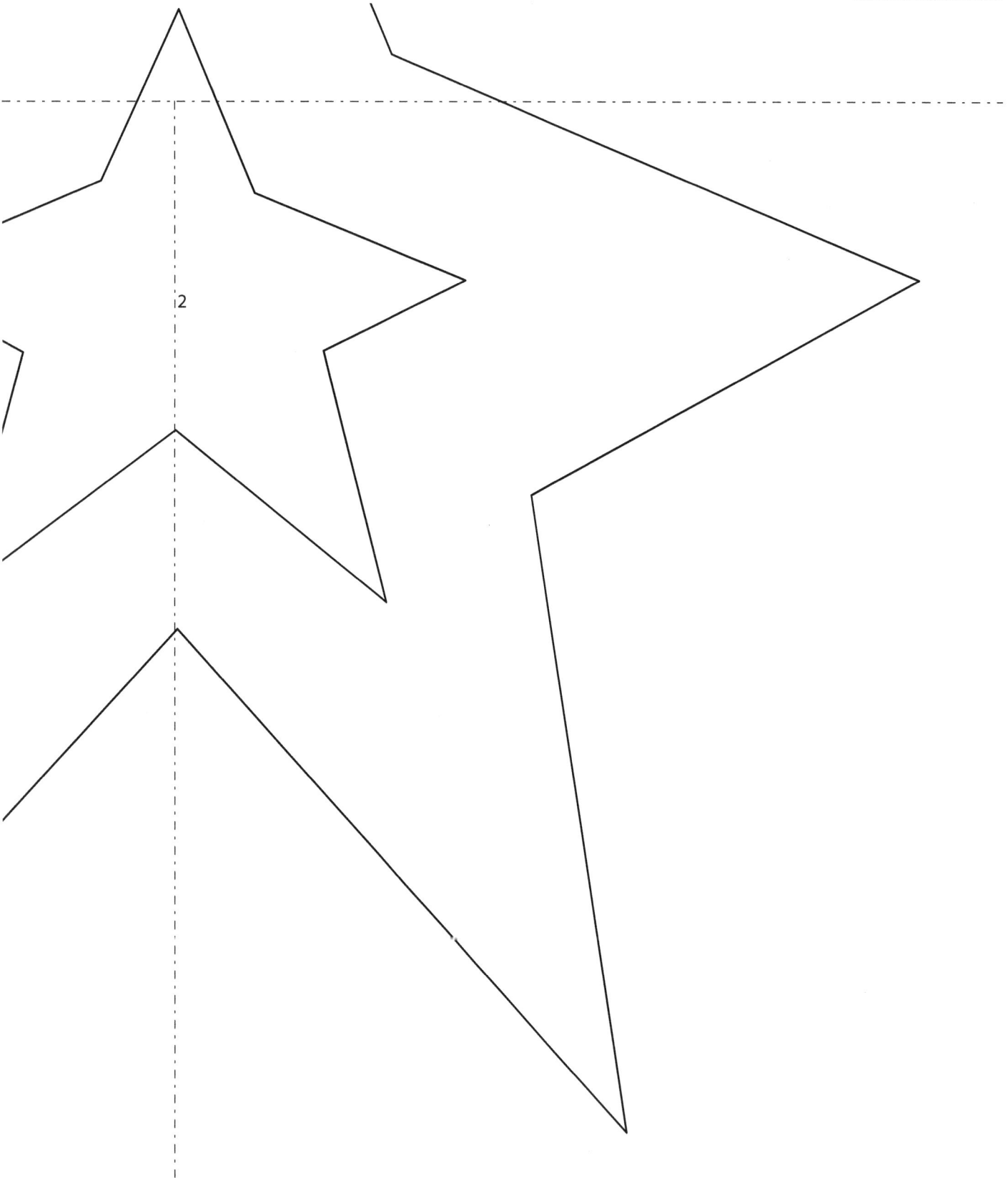

2

August

To make complete pattern, join the following
pages, following the diagram for reference.

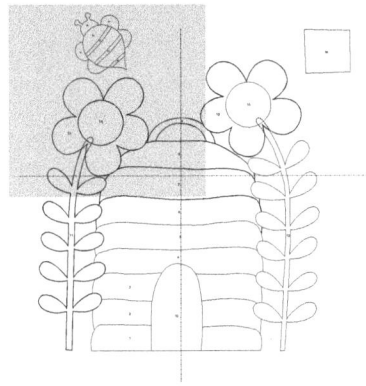

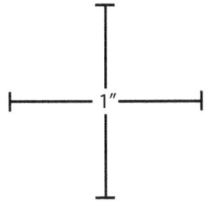

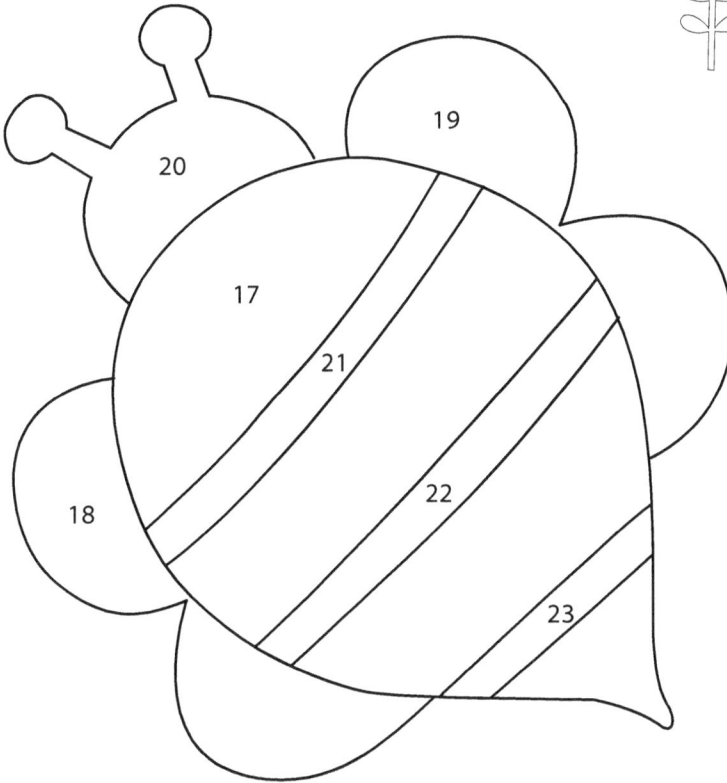

1"

19

20

17

21

18

22

23

14

13

9

8

7

1

August

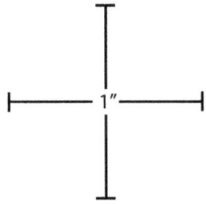

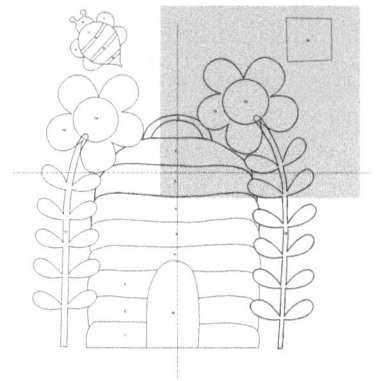

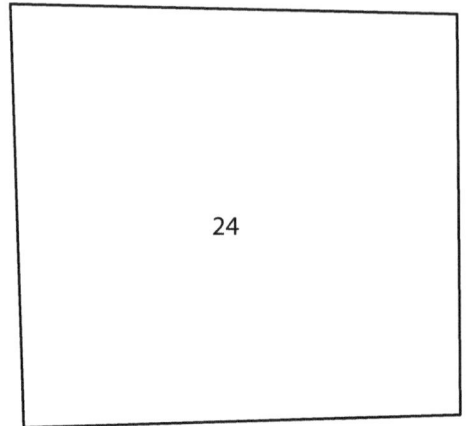

24

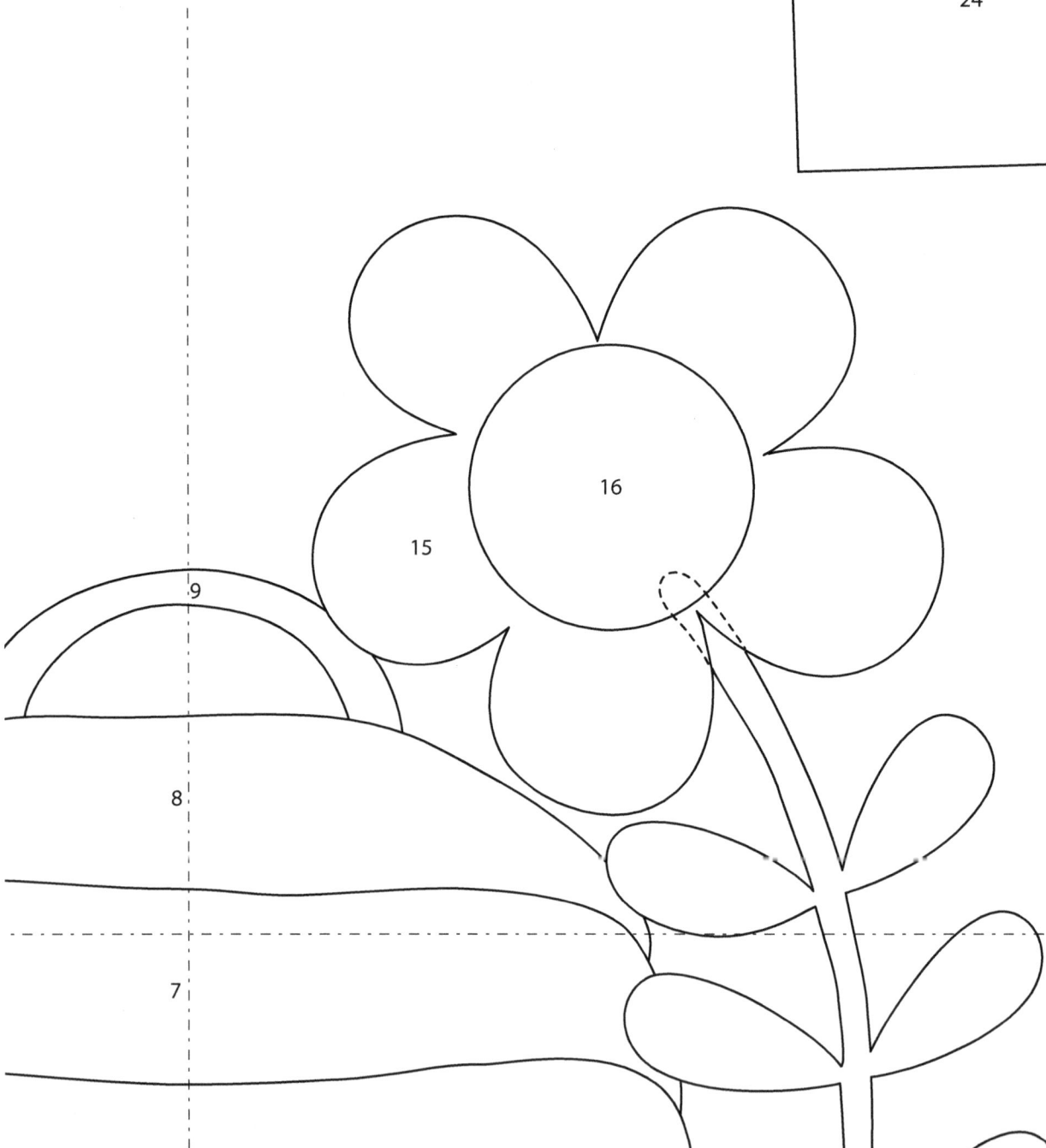

16

15

9

8

7

August

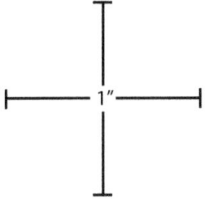

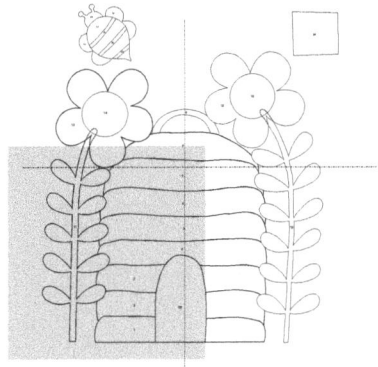

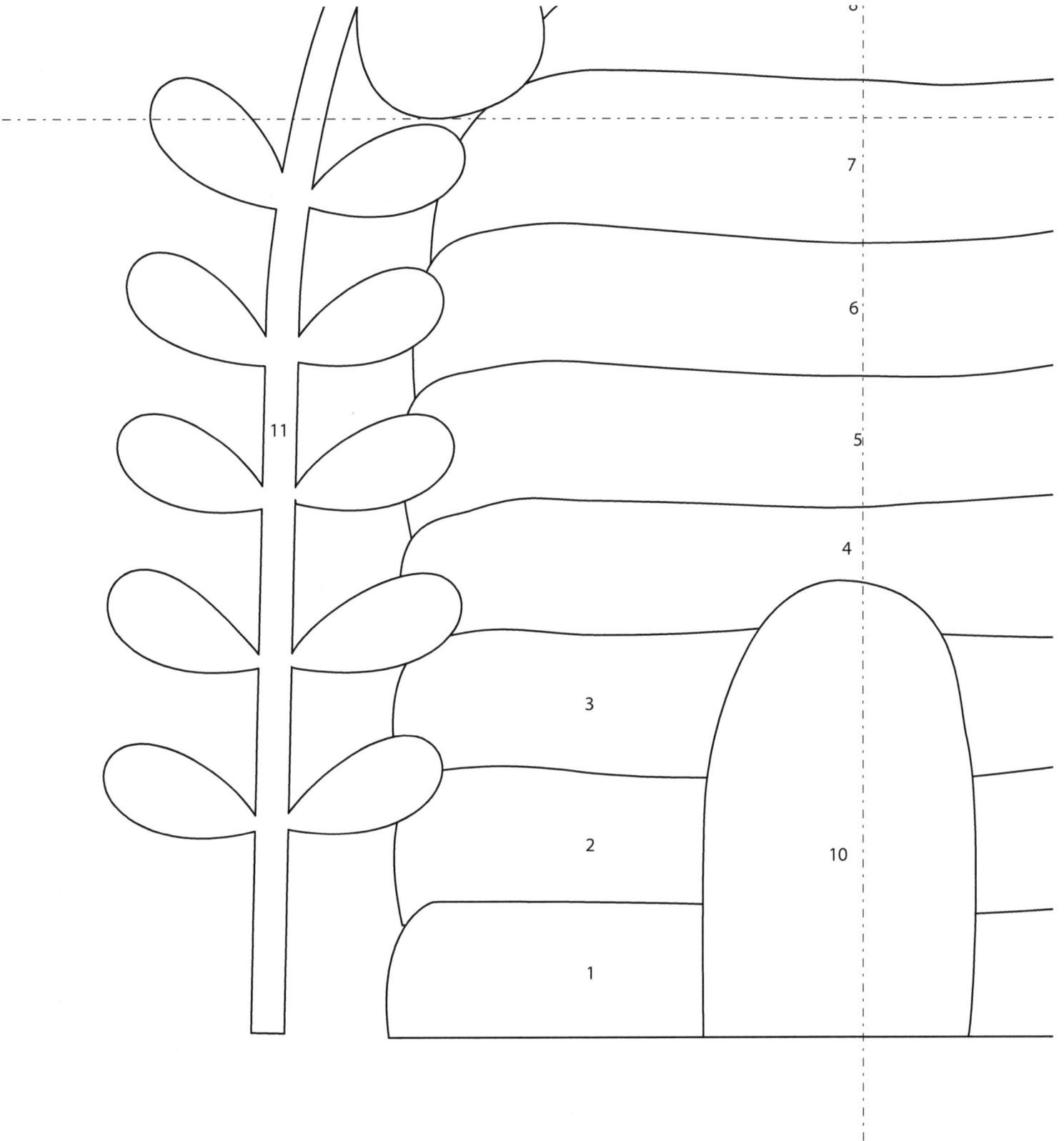

August

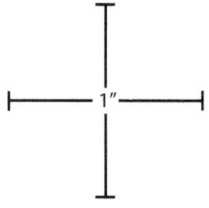

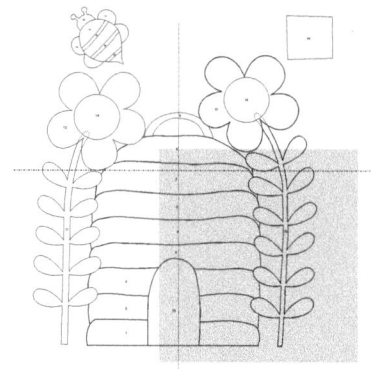

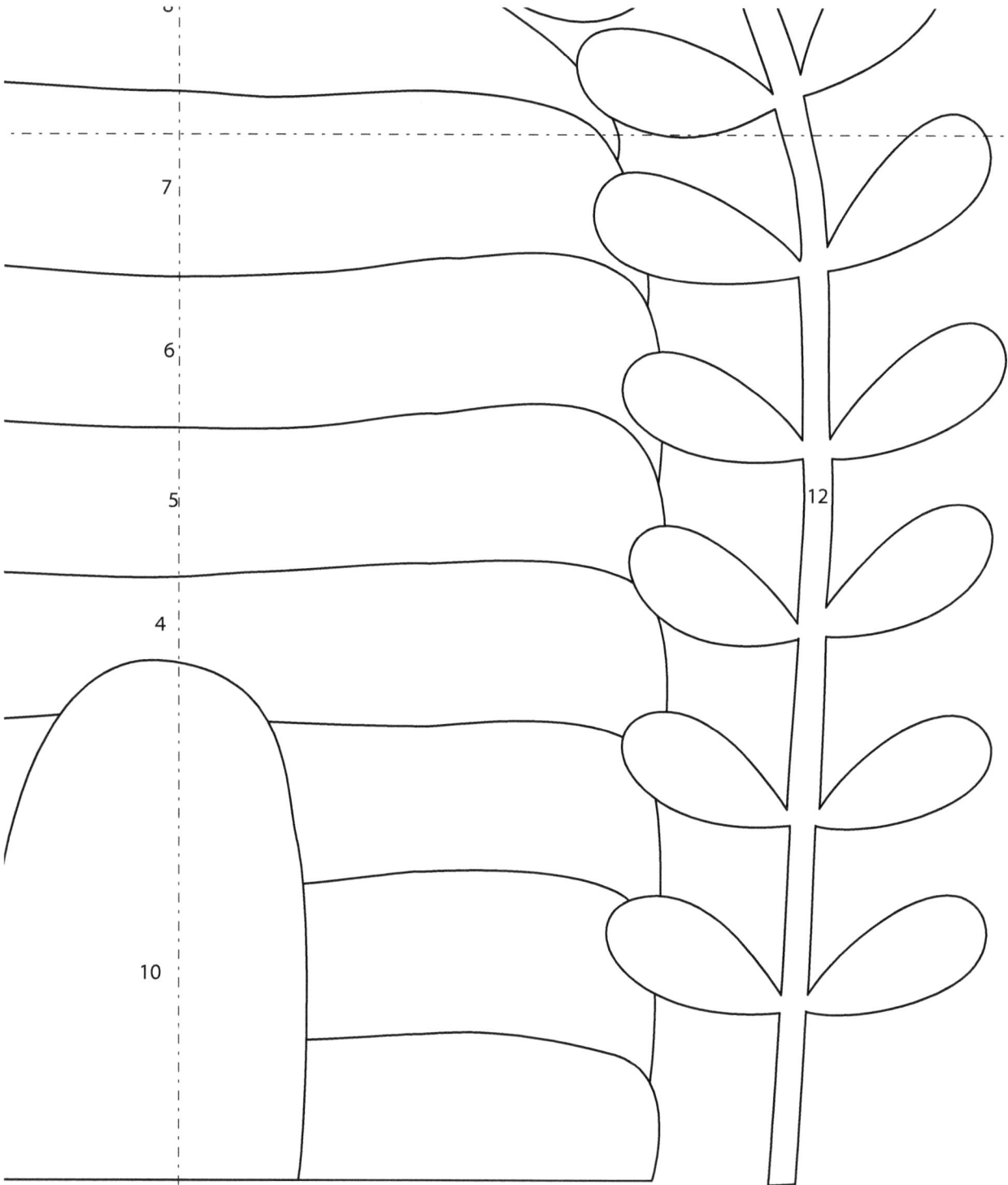

7

6

5

4

10

12

September

1"

To make complete pattern, join the following
pages, following the diagram for reference.

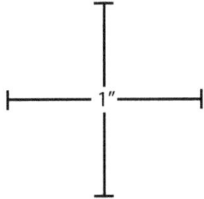

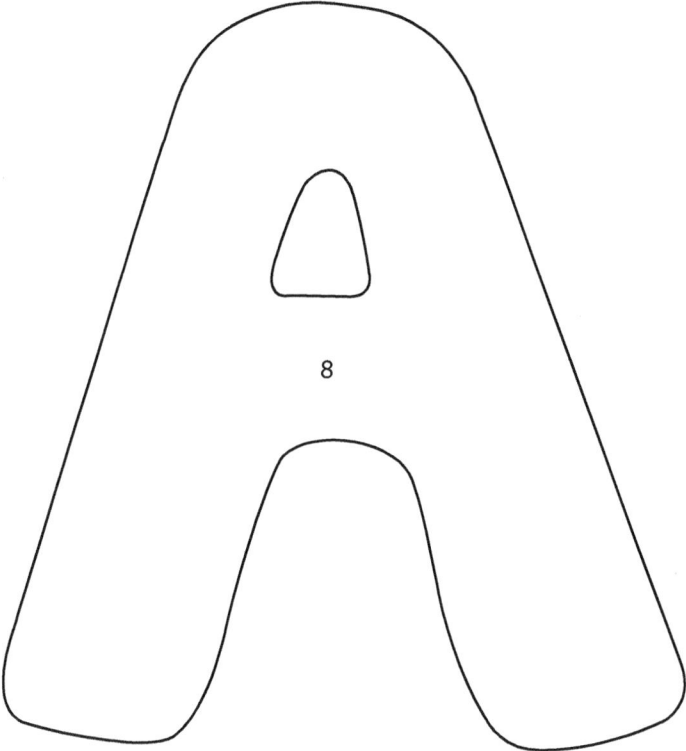

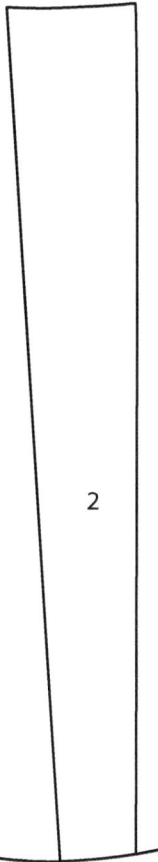

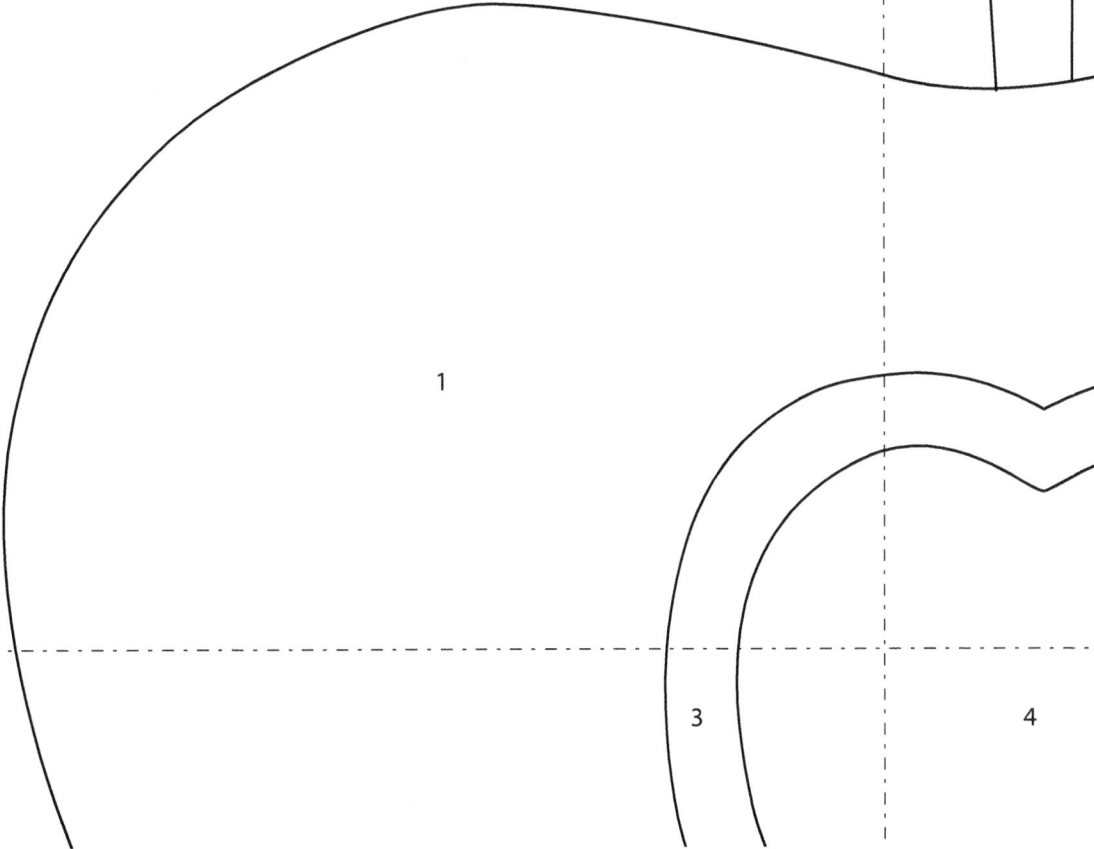

8

2

1

3

4

September

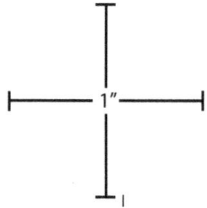

1"

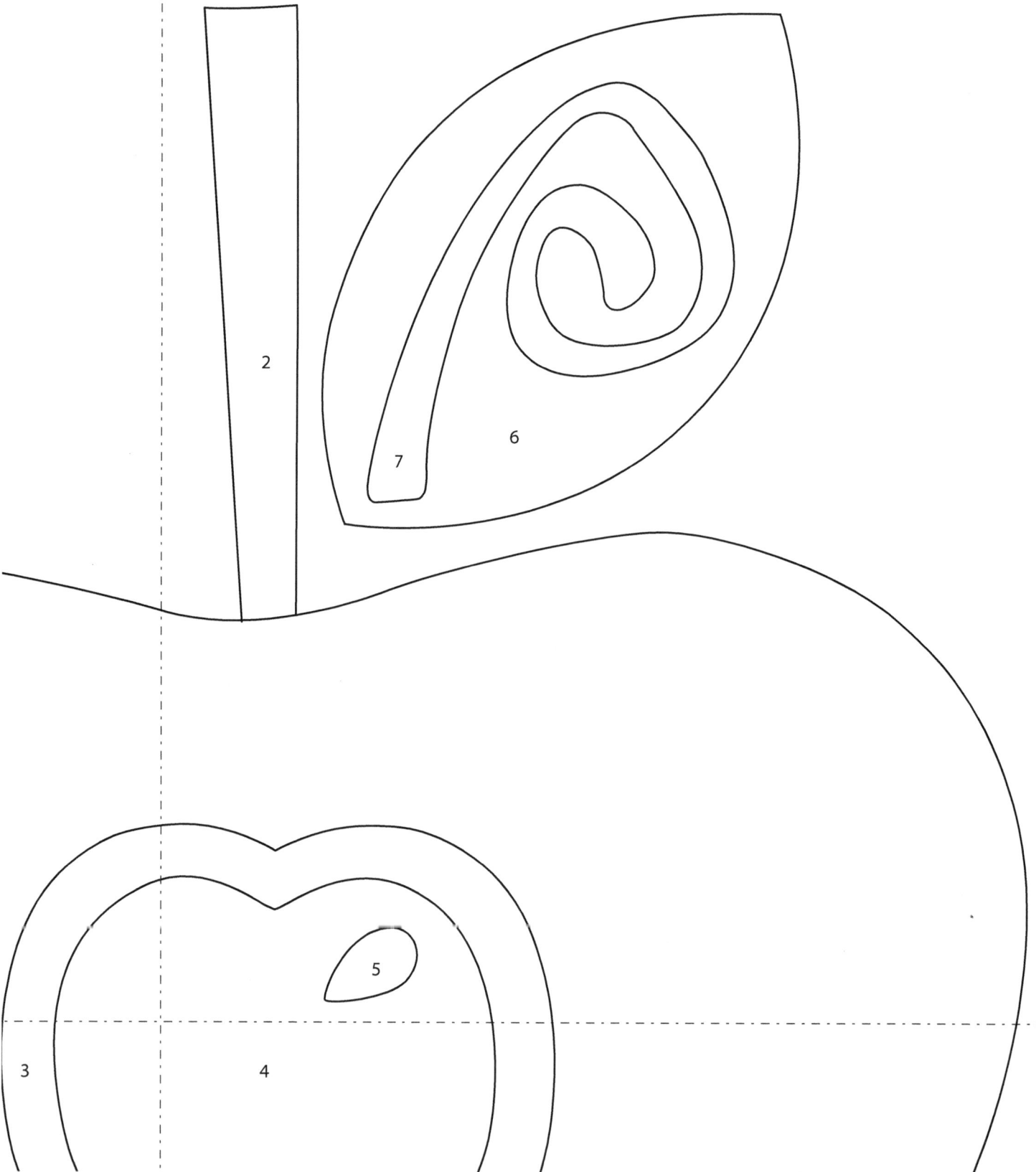

2

7

6

5

3

4

September

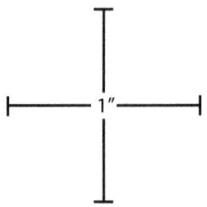

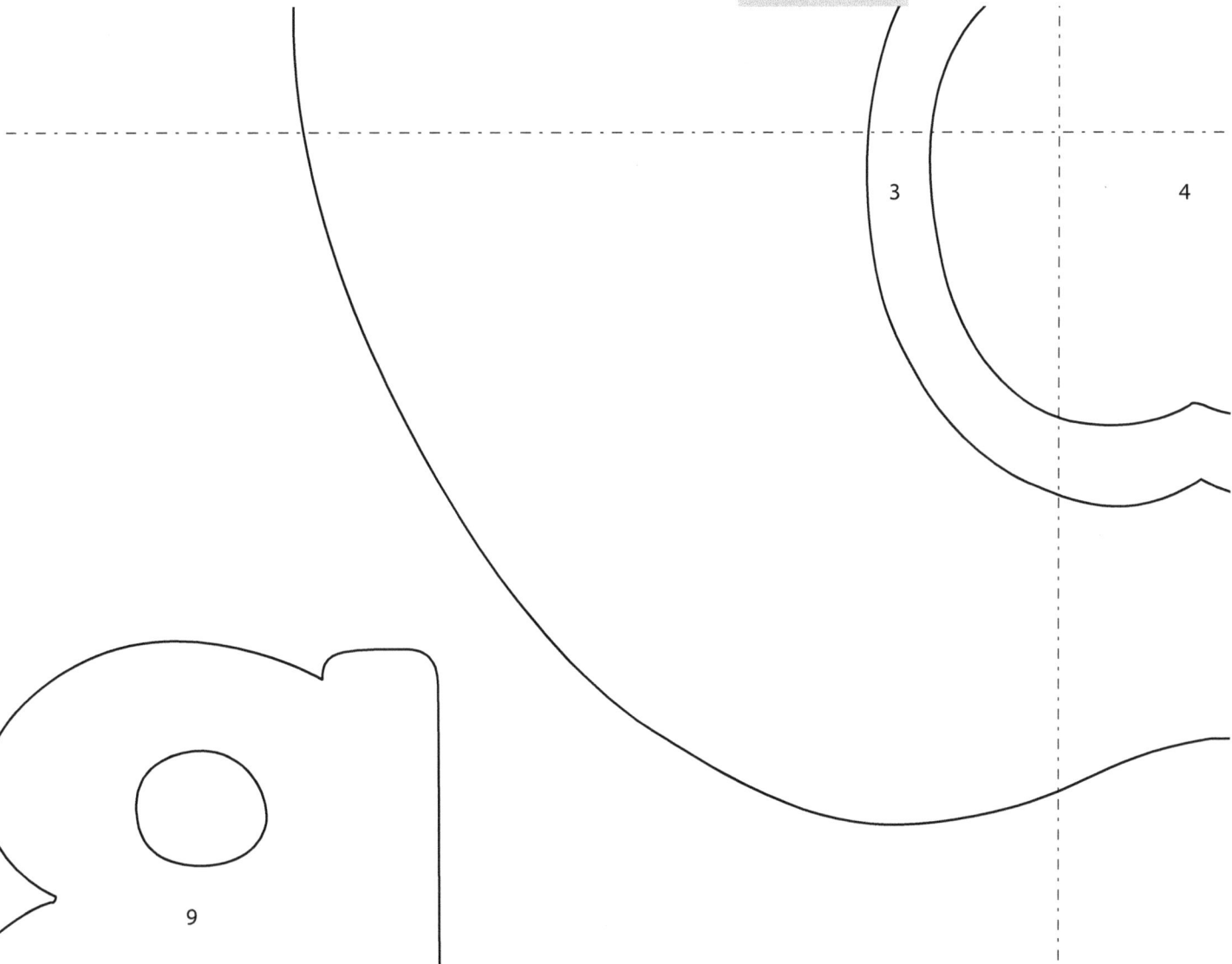

3

4

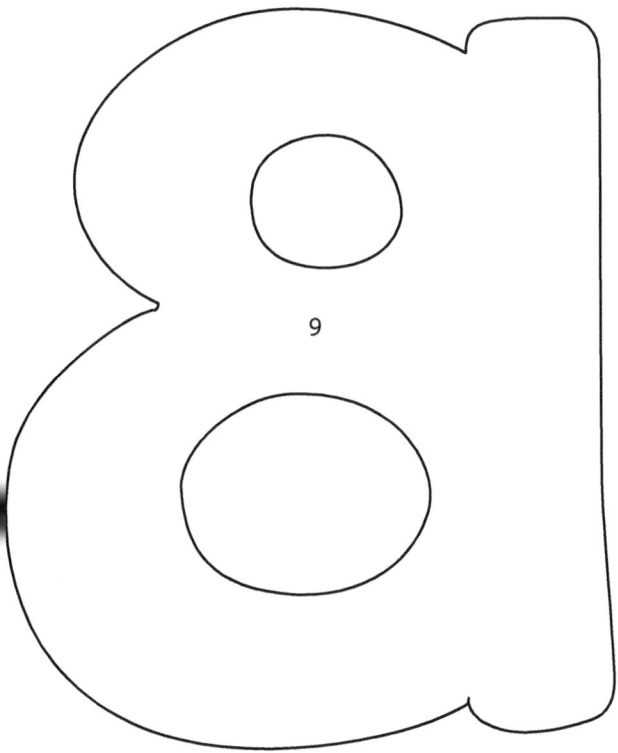

9

September

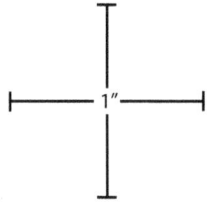

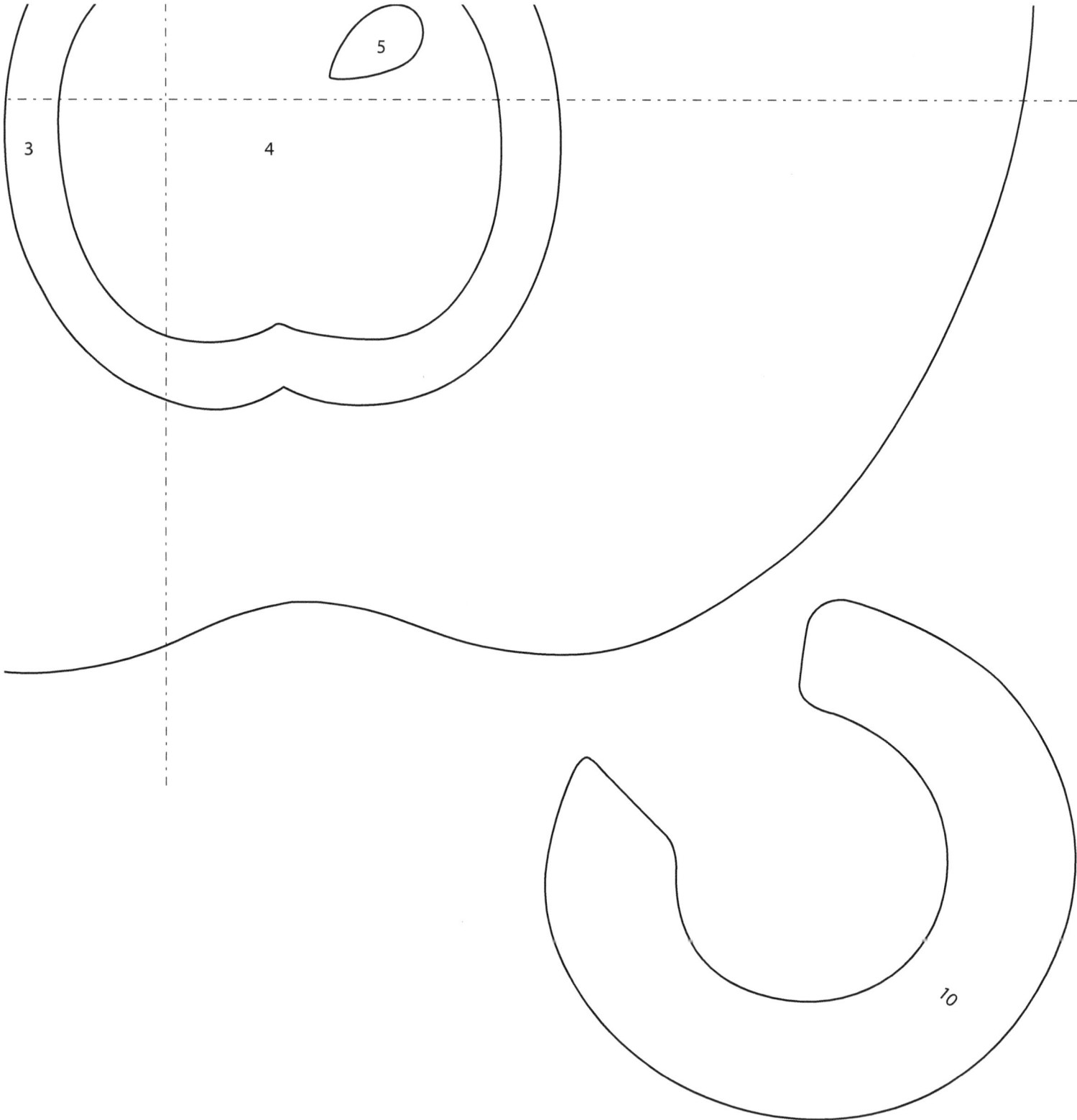

3

4

5

10

September

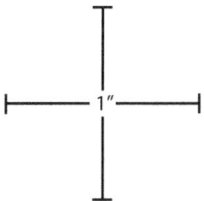

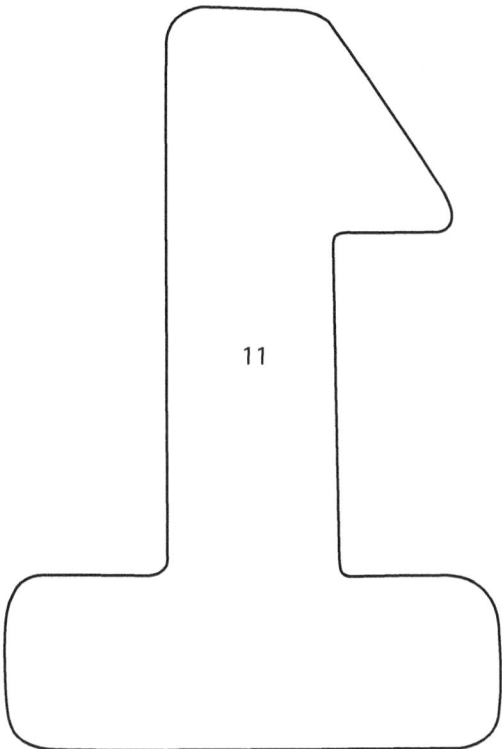

11

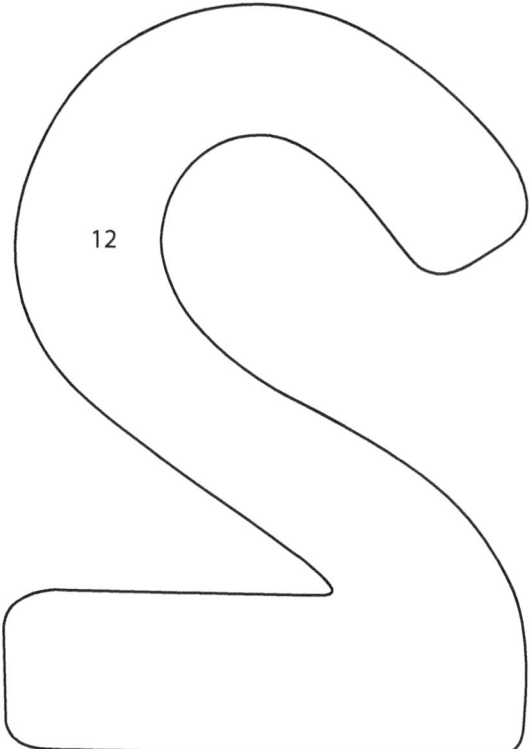

12

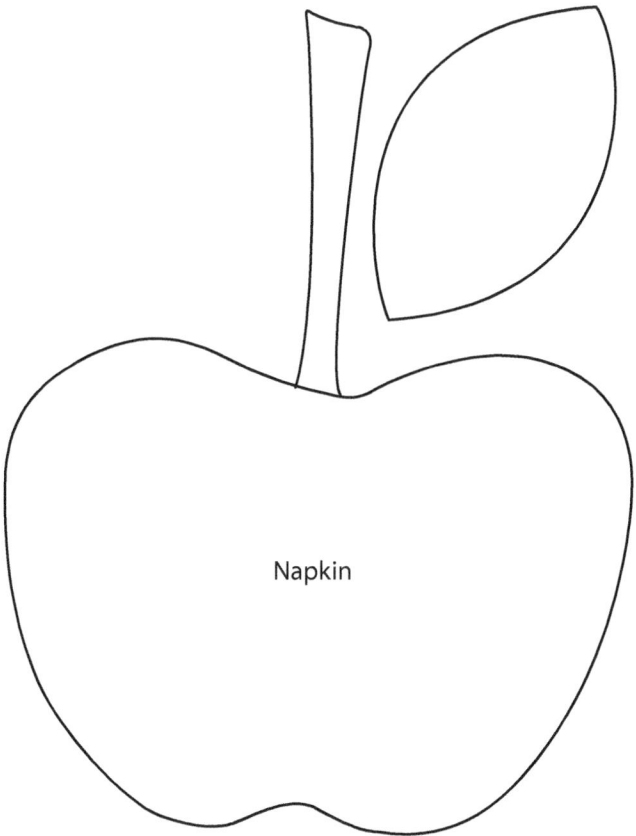

Napkin

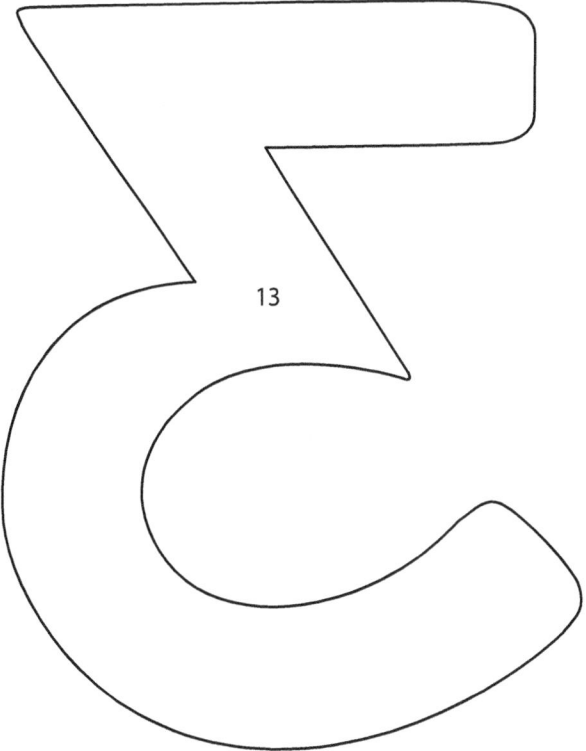

13

October

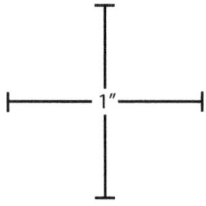

To make complete pattern, join the following pages, following the diagram for reference.

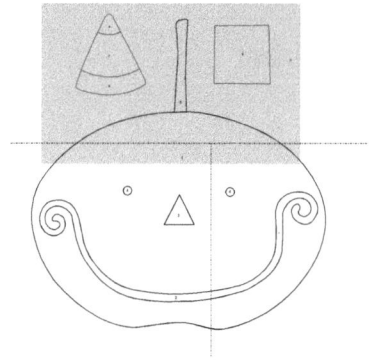

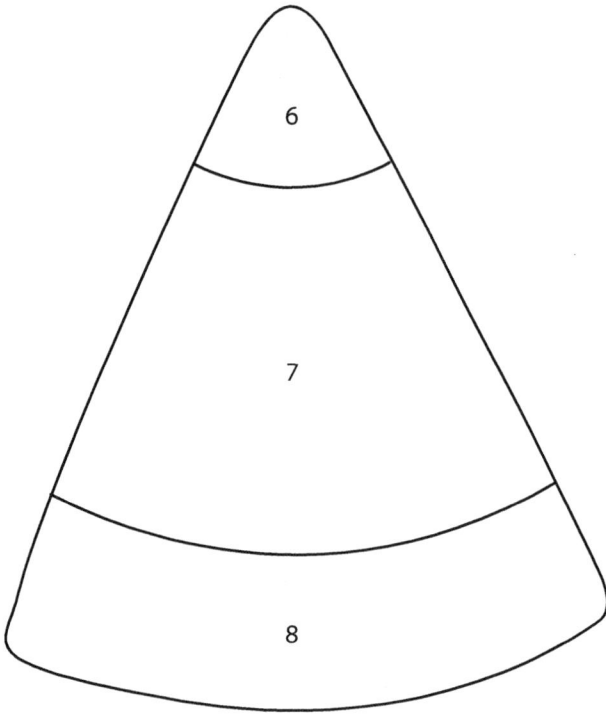

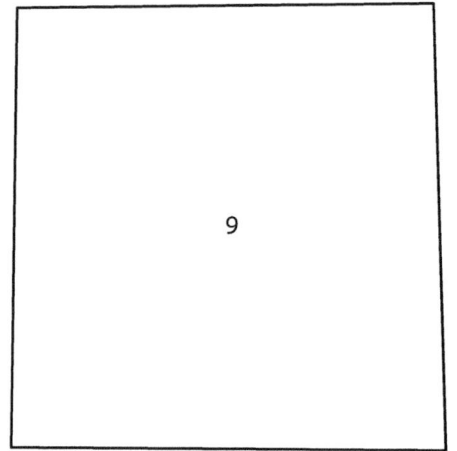

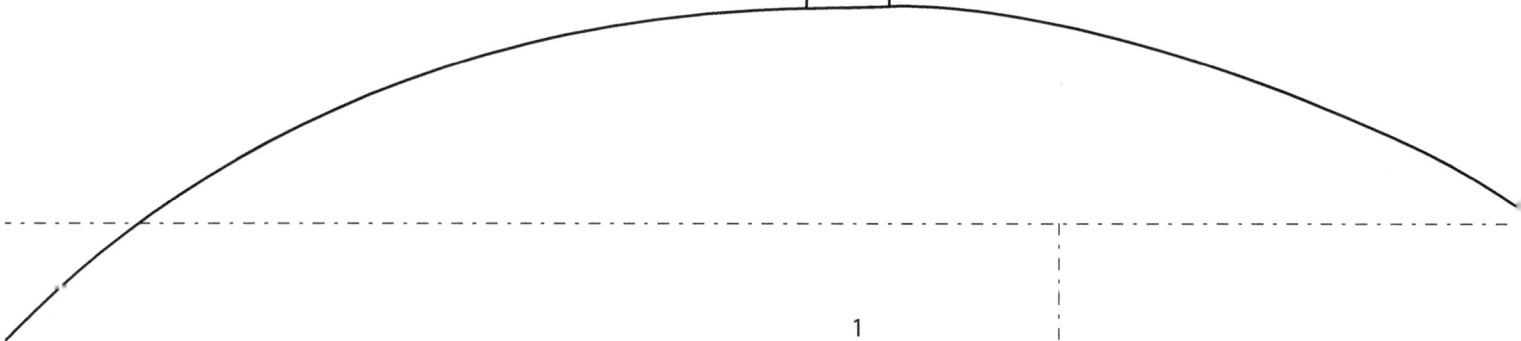

6

7

8

9

5

1

4

4

October

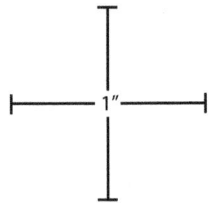

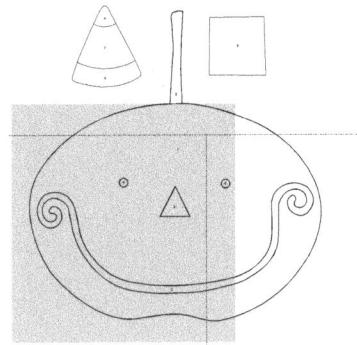

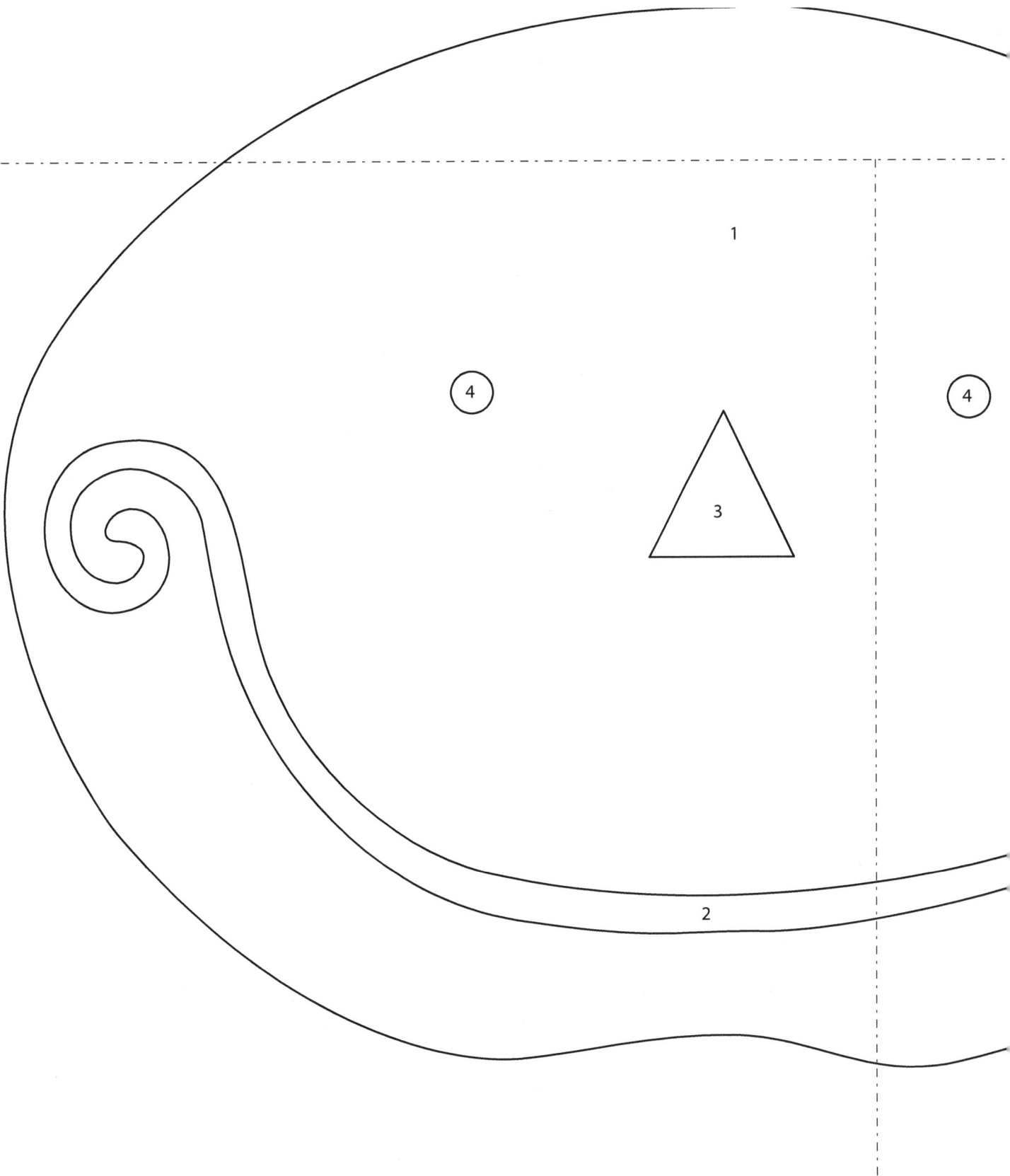

1

4

4

3

2

October

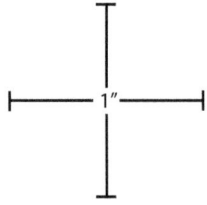

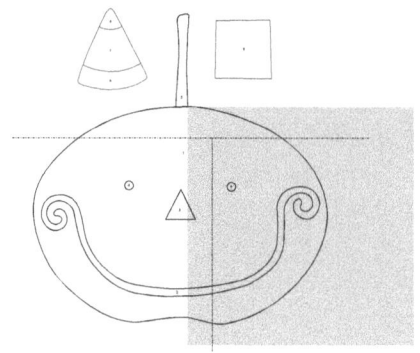

1

④

November

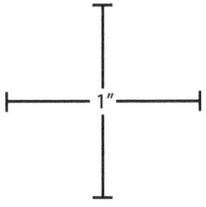

To make complete pattern, join the following pages, following the diagram for reference.

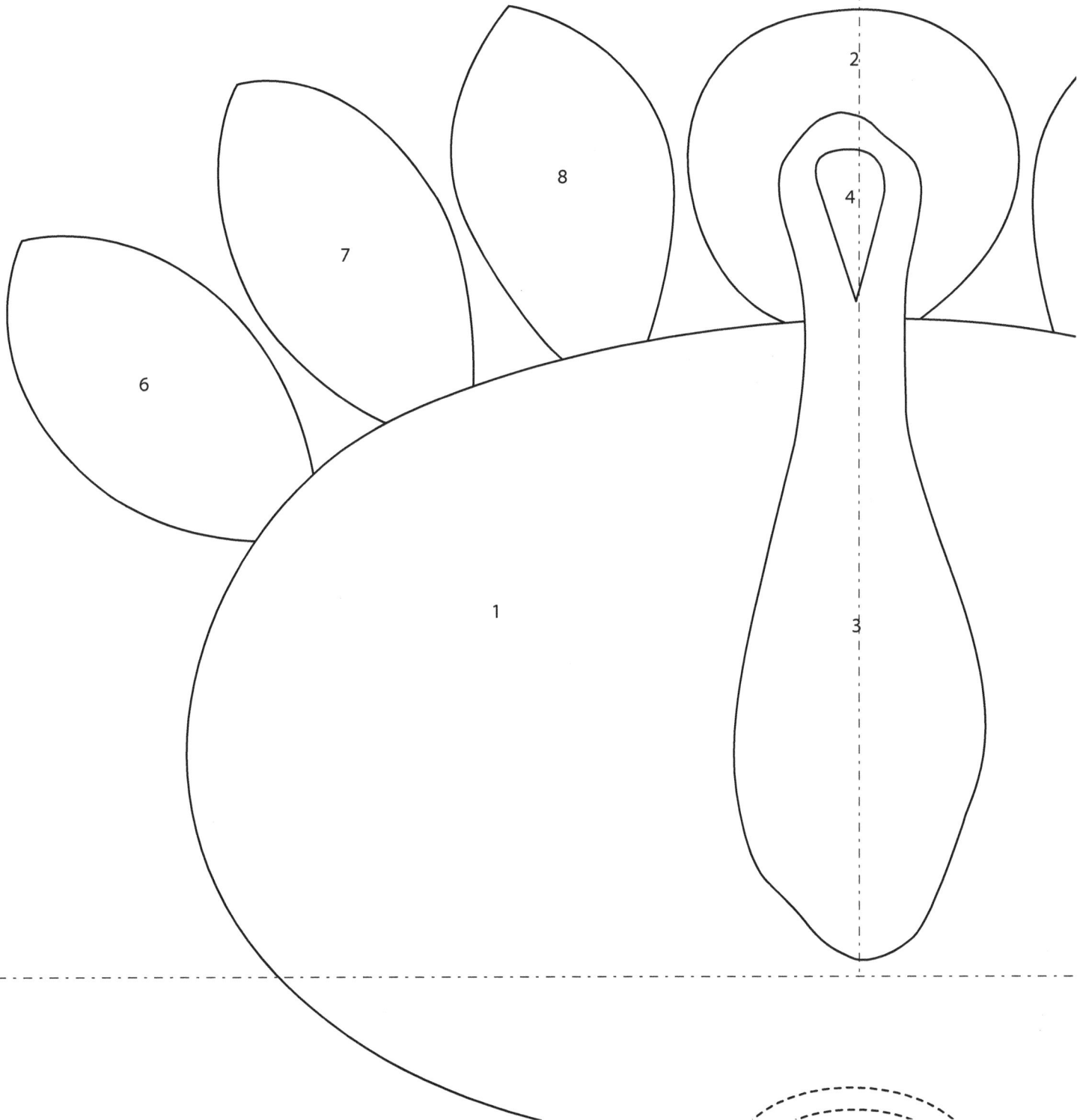

1"

2

8

7

4

6

1

3

November

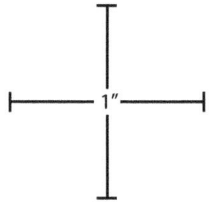

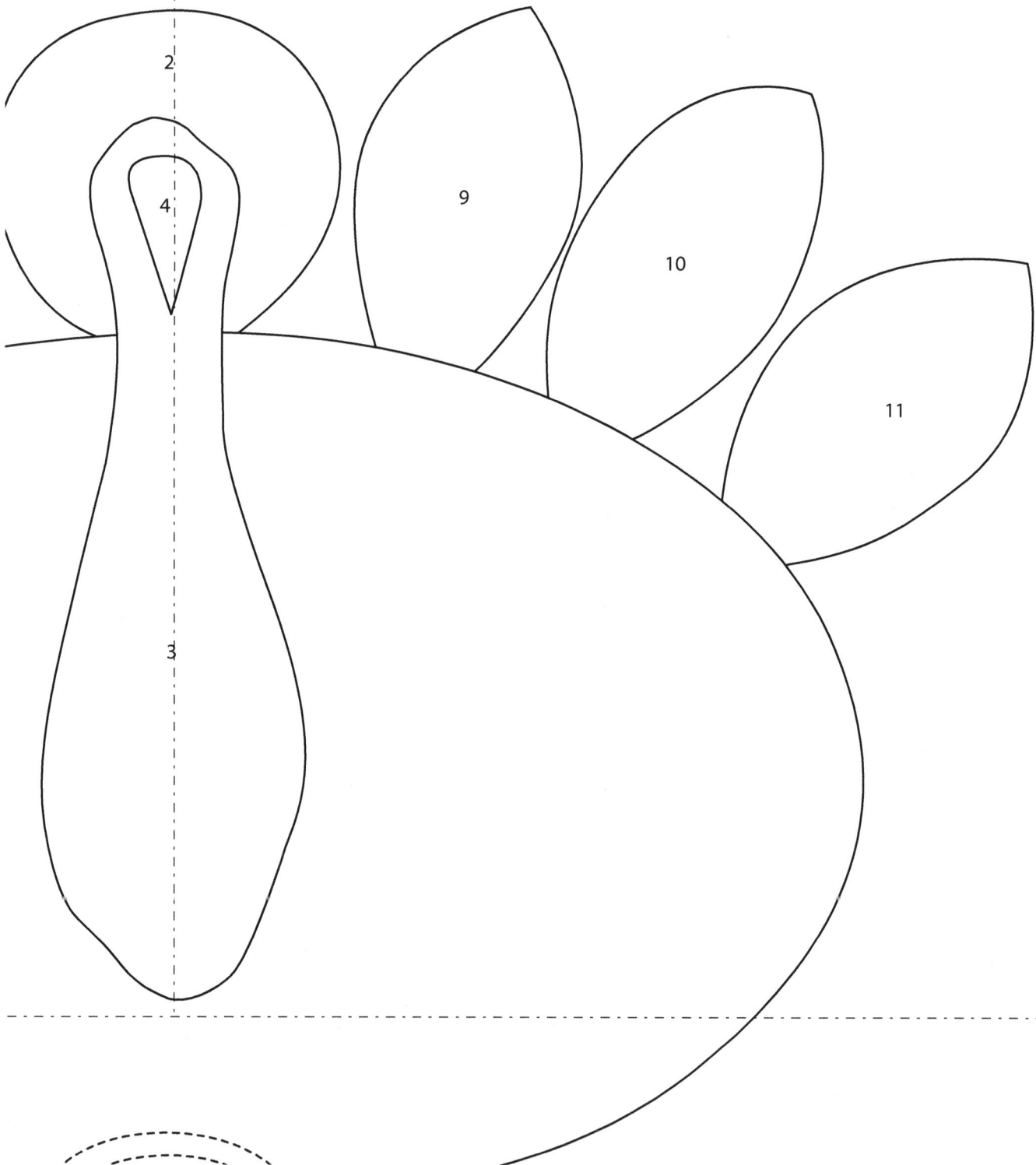

November

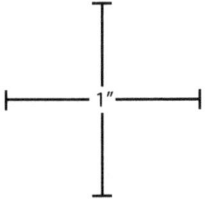

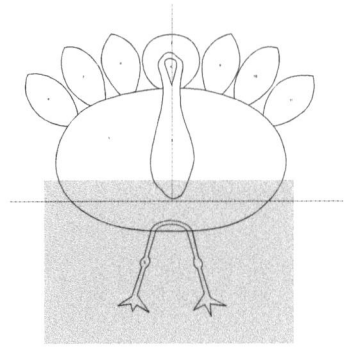

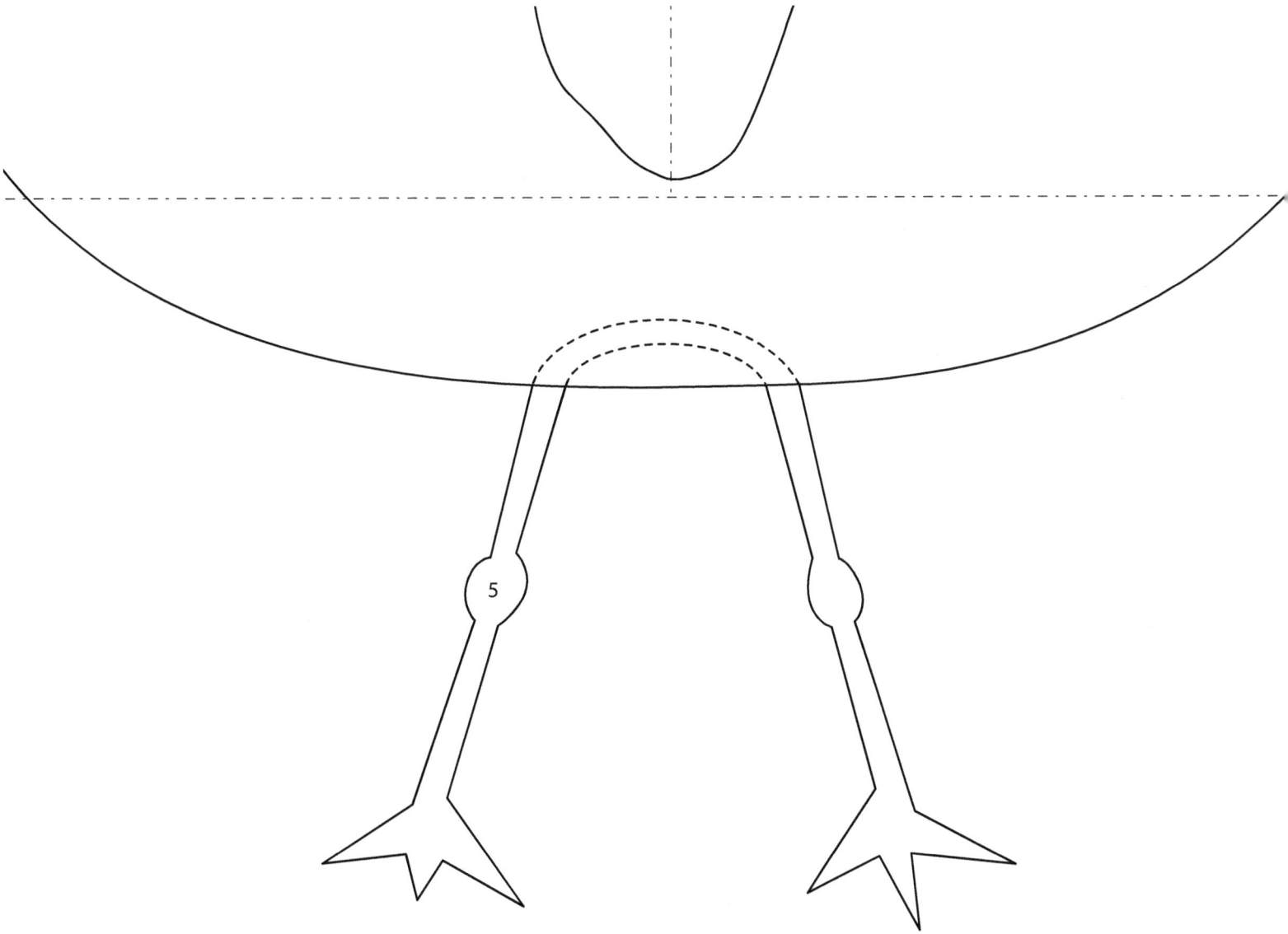

5

November

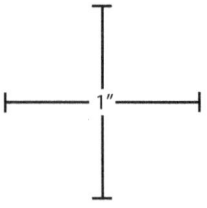

12

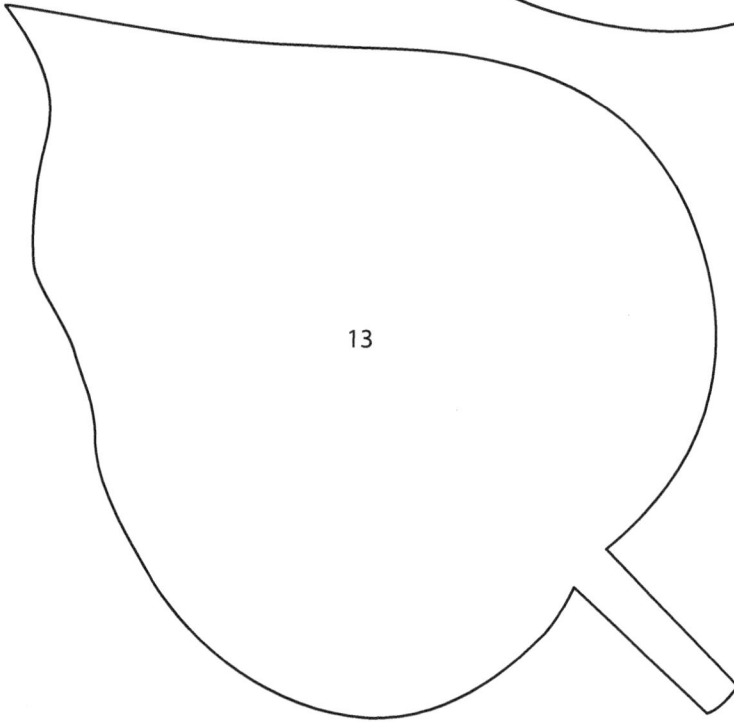

13

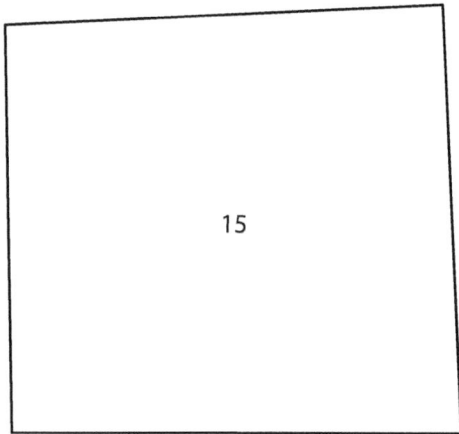

15

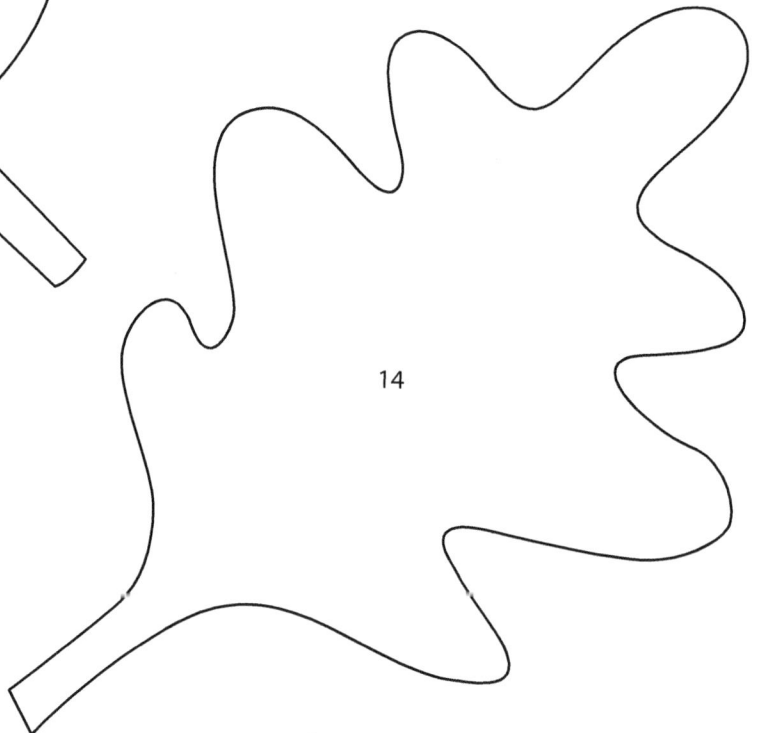

14

December

1"

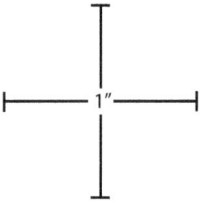

To make complete pattern, join the following
pages, following the diagram for reference.

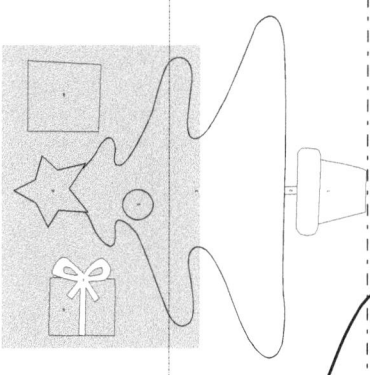

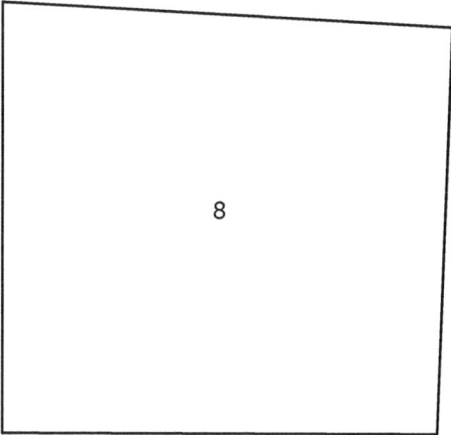

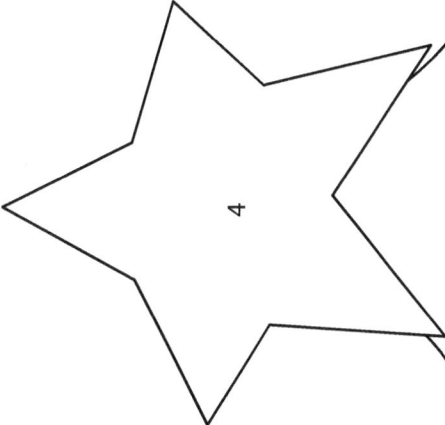

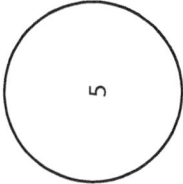

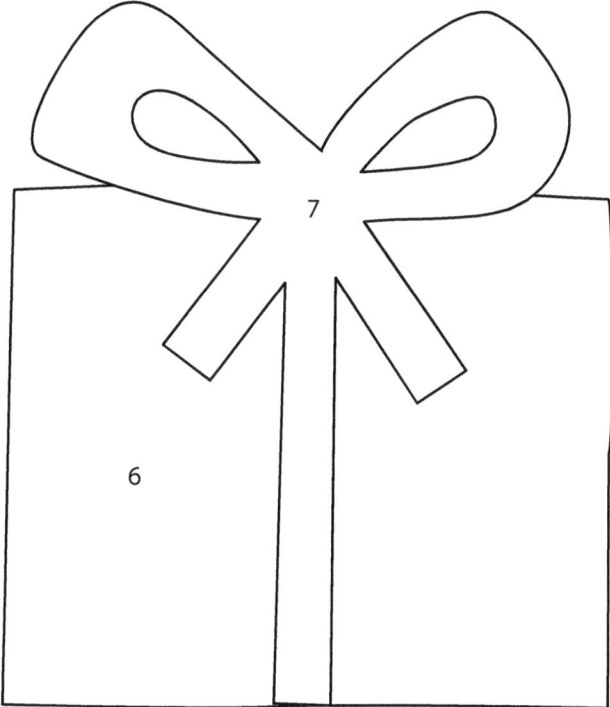

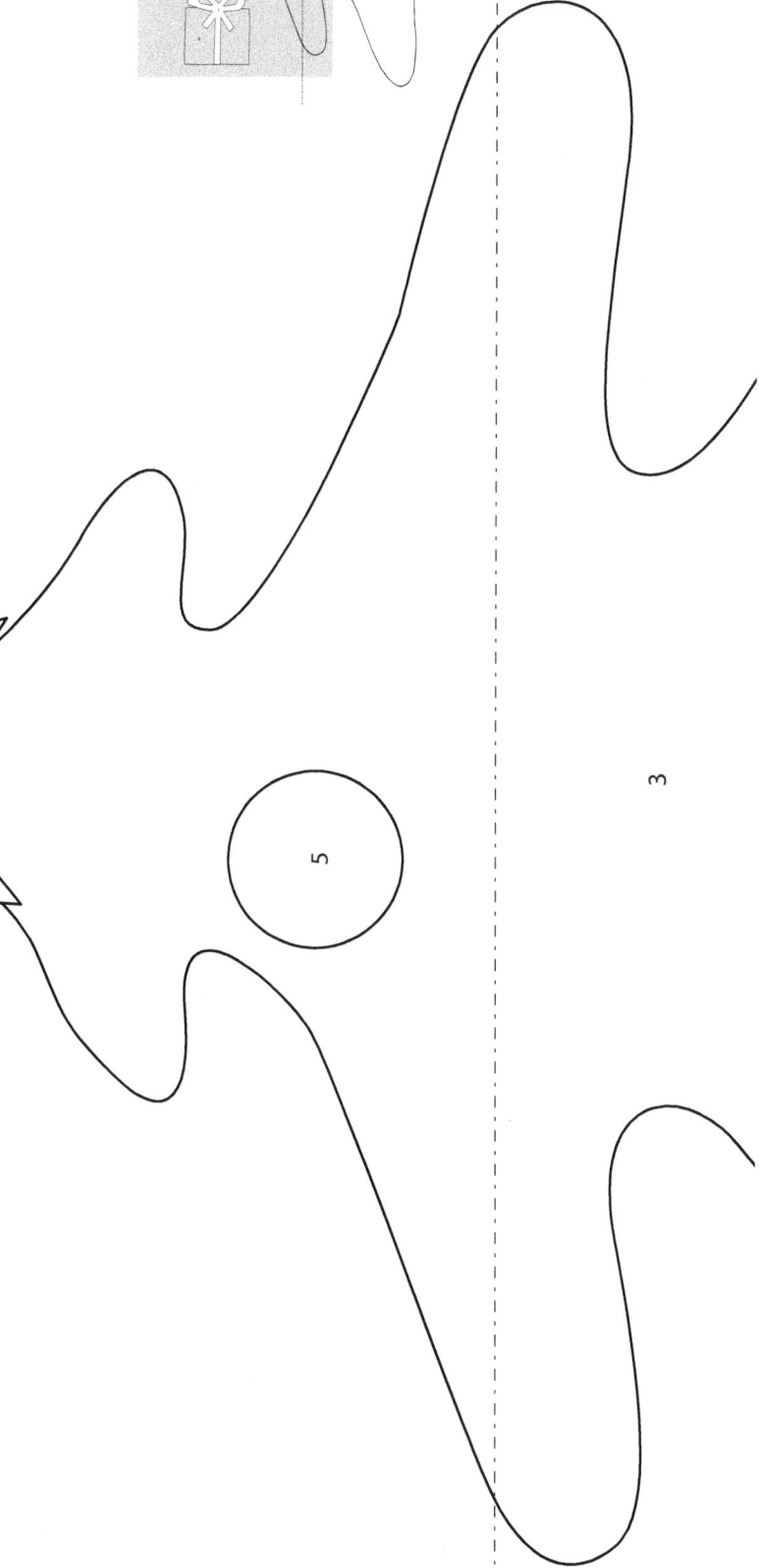

8

4

3

5

7

6

December

1"

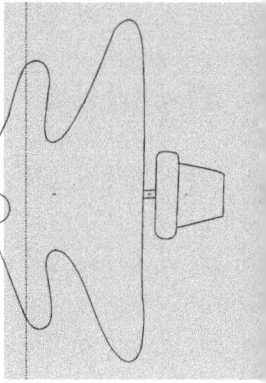

5

3

2

1

About the Author

Kim Schaefer began sewing at an early age and was quilting seriously by the late 1980s. Her early quilting career included designing and producing small quilts for craft shows and shops across the country.

In 1996, Kim founded Little Quilt Company, a pattern company focused on designing a variety of small, fun-to-make projects.

In addition to designing quilt patterns, Kim is a best-selling author for C&T Publishing. Kim also designs fabric for Andover/Makower and works with Leo Licensing, which licenses her designs for nonfabric products.

Kim lives with her family in southeastern Wisconsin.

For more information on Little Quilt Company, please visit www.littlequiltcompany.com, which offers Kim's entire collection of patterns, books, and fabrics.

Little Quilt Company's Facebook page has posts about new patterns, books, and fabrics, and an occasional peek at Kim's latest work.

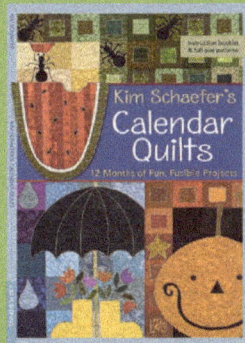

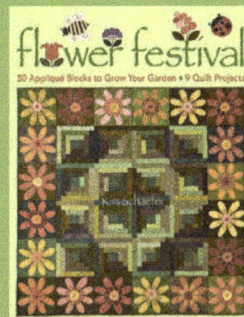

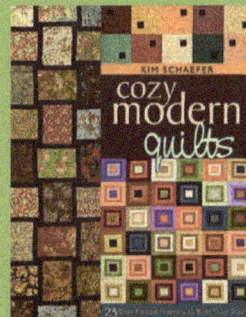

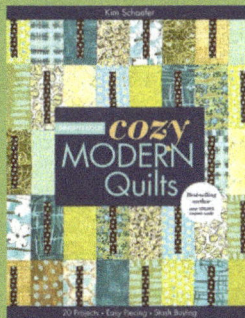

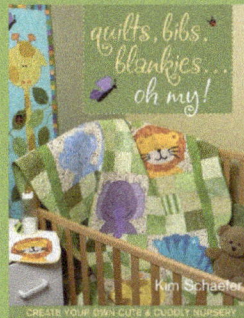

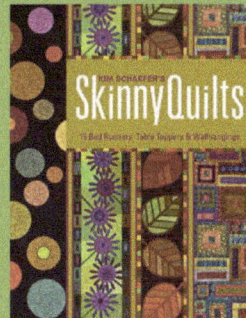

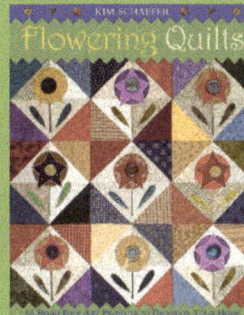

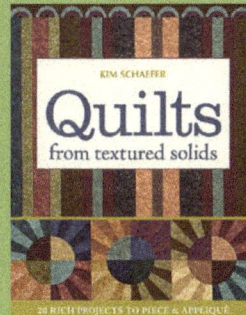

Available as an eBook only   Available as an eBook only

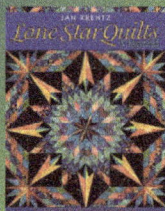

www.ingramcontent.com/pod-product-compliance
Lightning Source LLC
Chambersburg PA
CBHW061415090426
42742CB00026B/3479